Better Together

How Christians Can Be a Welcome Influence in Their Neighborhoods

Copyright © 2020 by Barna Group. All rights reserved.

ISBN: 978-1-945269-70-7

All information contained in this document is copyrighted by Barna Group and shall remain the property of Barna Group. U.S. and international copyright laws protect the contents of this document in their entirety. Any reproduction, modification, distribution, transmission, publication, translation, display, hosting or sale of all or any portion of the contents of this document is strictly prohibited without written permission of an authorized representative of Barna Group.

The information contained in this report is true and accurate to the best knowledge of the copyright holder. It is provided without warranty of any kind: express, implied or otherwise. In no event shall Barna Group or its respective officers or employees be liable for any special, incidental, indirect or consequential damages of any kind, or any damages whatsoever resulting from the use of this information, whether or not users have been advised of the possibility of damage, or on any theory of liability, arising out of or in connection with the use of this information.

Scripture quotations are taken from the Holy Bible, New Living Translation, copyright ©1996, 2004, 2015 by Tyndale House Foundation. Used by permission of Tyndale House Publishers, a Division of Tyndale House Ministries, Carol Stream, Illinois 60188. All rights reserved.

Funding for this research was made possible by the generous support of Lutheran Hour Ministries. Barna Group was solely responsible for data collection, analysis and writing of the report.

Table of Contents

5   **Preface**
By Rev. Dr. Tony Cook

9   **Introduction**

12   **Contributor Panel**

15   **Welcome to the Neighborhood:**
Types of People Gathering for Community Impact

Keys for Organizing & Measuring Neighborhood Actions
A Q&A with Shawn Duncan, Donell Woodson & Monica Evans

Affective Learning: How Congregants Move from Passion to Action
By Rev. Dr. Jason Broge

37   **Why Community Groups Act:**
The Interests & Issues That Prompt Christians to Organize

Serving Neighborhoods Through Creativity
A Q&A with Makoto Fujimura

The Value of Local Learning & Listening
A Q&A with Greg Russinger

55 | **What Community Groups Achieve:**
An Overview of Dynamics & Outcomes

A Vision That Lasts
A Q&A with Ruth Evans

Cultural Trends Shaping Our Neighborhoods
A Q&A with Gabe Lyons

81 | **Inspiring Action:**
How Churches Nurture—and Release—People Who Want to Do Good

Navigating the Intersection of Church Leadership & Community Engagement
A Q&A with Becca Stevens

103 | **Conclusion**
Partnering with Churchgoers for Neighborhood Impact

Appendix
107 | **A. Notes**
109 | **B. Methodology**
113 | **C. Acknowledgments**
115 | **D. About the Project Partners**

Preface

by Rev. Dr. Tony Cook
Vice President of Global Ministries, Lutheran Hour Ministries
Executive Director, The Hopeful Neighborhood Project

In an increasingly polarized age where an "us vs. them" mentality can convince us that those unlike ourselves are of less worth, this project is anchored in the belief that every human being is knit together by the same God and, as such, has value—a gift from God with gifts to share.

This project affirms God as the giver of all good gifts, including the gifts of self, others and the community we share. Its goal is to encourage people to voluntarily and collectively use their God-given gifts, even if they don't recognize their source, for the common good of their neighborhoods, loving their neighbors as themselves and working together to imagine future possibilities. God-given possibilities.

This work is not about researching another church program. It's not about adding one more thing to the congregation's calendar. It's about unleashing our neighborhoods' God-given gifts in everyday life. As the Great Steward, God doesn't waste a single life experience. He knows our gifts and calls us to use them today, right where we live.

At Lutheran Hour Ministries, we have dedicated ourselves to equipping Christians around the world to gain a hearing for the gospel in natural and fruitful ways. In fact, the first study in our research partnership with Barna Group focused specifically on learning more about how Christians and non-Christians alike experience and engage in spiritual conversations. That research yielded important insights, helpful tools and resources, and an award-winning report, *Spiritual Conversations in the Digital Age*.

The following year, our research expanded from individuals engaged in spiritual conversations to the households in which they live. That report, *Households of Faith*, demonstrated that we don't live in isolation, but within a beautiful and complex network of relationships. It expanded our concept of our own households, pushing beyond the limits (and limitations) of our families of origin or the physical walls of our houses to explore how hospitality opens the door to faith formation and deepens connections.

Now, in part three of our partnership, we continue our journey from the individual, to the household and now into our neighborhoods and beyond. That's what this new research is all about. We have worked tirelessly with our partners at Barna to plumb the depths of questions such as:

- How do you build trust in communities where Christians and the Church don't have a great reputation?
- What possibilities exist in the gifts of community members?
- What motivates Christians to make a hopeful difference in their neighborhoods?

- What's the most fruitful way of connecting individual Christians with a heart for their neighbors to their community?
- What's the role of congregations and ministry leaders in this effort?

The results of this research have increased the excitement I first experienced when this multi-year project began. I now find myself wondering, what would happen in our increasingly polarized age if more and more Christians were inspired and equipped to embrace the gift of community we have been given? What if the Church became known as a source of hope and possibility rather than scorn? What if every Christian actively proclaimed the gospel of Jesus Christ in both word and deed, becoming a faithful and encouraging presence in their neighborhoods around the world?

My time spent in partnership with Barna has convinced me that there is a faithful path forward revealed within this research. It's not, however, just another program or cookie-cutter solution. It's a vision of hope based on the acknowledgement of what God has done and is doing in and through our neighborhoods. As a result, I and Lutheran Hour Ministries are committing ourselves to applying this research, to taking the step we are asking you to consider, by creating The Hopeful Neighborhood Project. I invite you to read on and join us in this exciting research. And when you are done, visit us at www.hopefulneighborhood.org to join us in the journey—for in the end, we are truly better together.

Your brother in Christ,
Tony Cook

Introduction

Over recent decades, much of Barna Group's research on the state of Christianity could be summarized like this: The Church in the United States has a reputation problem.

This seems especially obvious as we look toward the future, examining perceptions among younger generations both inside and outside the Church. In research for his book *Faith for Exiles*, Barna president David Kinnaman found that the percentage of young adults with a Christian background who have dropped out of church continues to climb, from 59 percent in 2011 to 64 percent in 2018.[1] In a recent international study of 18–35-year-olds, about one-third of young adults from 25 countries, including the U.S., says terms like "hypocritical," "judgmental" and "anti-homosexual" describe present-day Christianity "a lot." To Millennials, even those who are practicing Christians (47%), the practice of evangelizing is often considered morally wrong.[2] Meanwhile, among the leading edge of Gen Z, religious affiliation in general is on the decline; granted, those in this age range are still in the formative years of developing their belief systems, but at this point the percentage of atheists in this generation doubles that of the general population (13% vs. 6% of all adults).[3]

What might change people's minds about the value of faith and the credibility of Christianity?

Multiple Barna studies suggest that, while public opinions about the Church at large are mixed (at best), feelings toward individual Christians are often much warmer. Redeeming the Church's broader reputation may need to involve recommitting to its personal presence—that is, as a locally embodied faith that knows and cares for the church's members and surrounding community. Consider this: The same international Barna study that shows young adults see Christianity as judgmental and hypocritical also reveals that friends and opportunities to fight injustice are the top things missing from this generation's experiences in communities of worship. However, that doesn't mean people aren't seeking out these connections and opportunities elsewhere or on their own—and it doesn't mean the Church can't step up now to play a part in facilitating them, even beyond formal ministry programs.

Barna undertook this study, alongside our research partners at Lutheran Hour Ministries (LHM), to learn more about the types of people, and particularly people of faith, who are taking initiative in their communities—who gather, donate, serve, create, teach, mobilize and innovate, alongside other passionate neighbors, to meet needs around them. In the first two reports released through our ongoing research partnership with LHM—*Spiritual Conversations in the Digital Age* and *Households of Faith*—we looked at the ways in which people form and express their faith in their daily lives and within their spheres of influence. This study looks at the next concentric circle of influence, from the individual to the household and now to the local community.

Specifically, this project seeks to understand Christians who are *being* the Church and loving their neighborhoods of their own volition, even outside of professional obligation or the formal structure of ministry programs. As the following chapters will detail, there are many forms these groups may take and many goals they may be working toward. The researchers have categorized participants of these groups

> Redeeming the Church's broader reputation may need to involve recommitting to its personal presence

to learn more about some of their motivations, how they organize and what's working.

Done and supported well, the possible benefits of such groups are not hard to imagine: fulfilling the Christian call to care for those in need, inspiring believers to take ownership of their faith, adding and growing new disciples, distributing personal responsibility when organizations have limited resources and reach, alleviating burdens for ministries and pastors who may be stretched thin already, deepening and improving the relationships and reputation of Christians, activating new or young leaders, and extending the reach of the Church beyond the institution while also strengthening membership within it. These could be much-needed solutions, both spiritual and practical, to questions about the Church's credibility and longevity in a secularizing age.

If you're a pastor reading this, perhaps this is not a new idea to you. The data indicate that many church leaders are in favor of giving church members and lay leaders some agency in living out the gospel on a local level in their own ways—though perhaps pastors have not focused on, invested in or measured this valuable effort yet. In this study, more than four out of five pastors tell Barna they prefer lay initiatives to new church programs (40% agree strongly, 52% agree somewhat), and more than two-thirds (68%) strongly agree that healthy ministries are ones in which lay people take more responsibility. Even so, only about one in 10 (9% strongly agree) is confident that their church is good at developing new leaders.

This report is intended to help churches understand the impact and inner workings of groups of good neighbors, and to help leaders develop a vision for how these members might complement their ministry goals for discipleship, growth and outreach. We hope that pastors, equipped with this research, might be able to move the members of their congregation from concern to action and, in the process, realize the power of releasing Christians to do good in their own neighborhoods.

> This project seeks to understand Christians who are *being* the Church and loving their neighborhoods of their own volition

Contributor Panel

Scattered throughout this report are quotes from a panel of expert contributors who took time to sit down with Barna Group and share from their own experiences working with community groups and organizations. We're very grateful for their insights, which gave us further opportunity to learn how such groups form, how they work and what makes them effective.

"Let's Talk About" Panel

Shawn Duncan
Director at
the Lupton Center

Monica Evans
Project manager at
the Lupton Center

Ben Allin
Coordinator of Intown
ESL4Peace, community
outreach manager &
intercultural / interreligious
peacebuilder at iface.org

Ruth Evans
Executive director
at Unite

Glenn Barth
President at GoodCities

Emily Hendren
Product owner at
Thrivent Action Teams

Joy Harty
Board member and
wife of co-founder
Scott Harty at Sixty Feet

Lynn Heatley
Executive director at
Love Riverside

Scott Kauffman
Content partner at Praxis

Greg Russinger
Co-founder
of Laundry Love

Kitti Murray
Founder & CEO
of Refuge Coffee Co.

Stephanie Wieber
Director of City Gospel
Movements at
Luis Palau Association

Contributor Panel • 13

Who Is Better Together?

Barna analyzed a custom segmentation, with a focus on practicing Christians, to learn more about individuals who are engaging meaningfully with their neighborhoods. Here's an introduction to three groups you'll get to know throughout this report.

ONE IN FOUR PRACTICING CHRISTIANS IS A…
COMMUNITY PARTICIPANT

Adults who have taken initiative to gather with multiple people multiple times for some level of local influence

Going Deeper
% among practicing Christian community participants

● **45 PERCENT OF COMMUNITY PARTICIPANTS ARE…**
COMPASSIONATE

Community participants who have connected with other members independently over their interests or a desire to change something or help others

● **30 PERCENT OF COMMUNITY PARTICIPANTS & 67 PERCENT OF COMPASSIONATE PARTICIPANTS ARE… COLLABORATIVE**

Compassionate participants who have been involved in a group where things were shared—passions, dues, decisions and so on—and the community was impacted

Practicing Christians

n=1,505 practicing Christian adults, July 25–August 15, 2019.
See the Methodology for more details about how these groupings were created.

Welcome to the Neighborhood:

TYPES OF PEOPLE GATHERING FOR COMMUNITY IMPACT

"We live in a world in which we need to share responsibility. It's easy to say, 'It's not my child, not my community, not my world, not my problem.' Then there are those who see the need and respond. I consider those people my heroes."
— *Fred Rogers*[4]

Though he passed in 2003, there has recently been much renewed interest in the life of Fred Rogers and his beloved children's television persona "Mister Rogers." Stories of his character have been shared under headlines declaring him "saintlike" or suggesting his example of compassion, curiosity and generosity might lead Americans through a divided era.[5] Memes bearing his famous quote about "looking for the helpers" are circulated whenever the public is trying to make sense of a natural disaster, shooting or other tragedy. Two films, both a documentary and a biopic, were released to great critical acclaim and tearful audiences.

What is it about Rogers that is posthumously striking such a chord? More than just nostalgic, much of his work speaks to deeply felt needs of our time. His faith was also as much a part of his career as his puppets or his sweaters; famously, he was ordained as a Presbyterian minister not for the pulpit but for his program.[6] For Christians especially, there are lessons in this—a primary one being that Rogers' values were never confined solely to his church or private life, but became central to his vocation, his sense of civic responsibility and his Neighborhood.

The message of *truly* knowing and loving one's community isn't just attractive; it calls us back to one of the strongest commands of Christ (Mark 12:31) and the reciprocal model of the early Church (Acts 2:42–47). This isn't an easy mandate to heed in a culture that, as Barna's own research and others' show, trends toward isolation, polarization and passivity. So, what does community-minded faith and action look like today?

In this chapter, we'll meet groups of people, including practicing Christians, who have seen needs and responded. They have taken it upon themselves to organize, create and serve—with others, across differences and for some level of local impact and influence. And they're doing so within and beyond the institutional Church.

Categorizing Participants

For the purposes of this study, the researchers defined and analyzed a series of participants who engage their communities. To begin winnowing down the sample while also still allowing for a variety of activities and outcomes, Barna decided to look at respondents we'll refer to as **community** participants, who, at some time in their adulthood, have had the following experiences in some kind of group, club or other association:

- Their participation was not required for their education or schooling.

> The message of *truly* knowing and loving one's community isn't just attractive; it calls us back to one of the strongest commands of Christ

- Their participation was not directly related to their job.
- The group included three or more people.
- The group met three or more times.
- The group provided some external benefit reaching beyond its own participants. Though those benefits might have extended widely, they had to have some local impact, meaning in one's own city or town. Additionally, while a church or Christian community could have benefited, it could not have been the *only* beneficiary of the group's actions.

With these guidelines in place, researchers' goal was to focus on people who might have been members of groups that were voluntarily joined without a sense of obligation, were not exclusively tied to a church program or had some positive impact outside the gathering itself in the neighboring community. By these requirements, about one in five in the total sample has participated in this type of gathering, including one-quarter of practicing Christians (26%) and 14 percent of all others.

As you can see, involvement in such associations is already relatively rare, but Barna further defined the spectrum of activity to isolate certain motivations or methods. In addition to community participants in the broadest grouping outlined above, we'll examine:

- **Compassionate** participants, who have been involved in at least one group that originated outside of an existing program offered at a church, school, civic or other institution and came together with others to do something they were interested in or passionate about, in order to change something or help someone or something.
- **Collaborative** participants, who, in addition to being compassionate, have been involved in at least one group where members

shared strong feelings or passions, resources (such as dues, tools or expertise), goals or decision-making abilities. Further, beyond the general prerequisite of having impact in their city or town, respondents had to specifically identify their community as a beneficiary of a group's efforts.

It's appropriate to think about these categories as a narrowing funnel, with one group feeding into the other. They are not exclusive. That is, all participants considered compassionate and collaborative must first meet the base requirements of being community participants, and all collaborative participants must first have the qualities of compassionate participants. Their common traits build upon one another so that, when we discuss collaborative actions, we're learning from an exemplary minority of organized, altruistic individuals who have contributed to outward-focused action in their communities.

These aren't always entirely new or independent efforts; four in 10 practicing Christians with experience in these groups (41% practicing

> We're learning from an exemplary minority of organized, altruistic individuals who have contributed to outward-focused action in their communities

n=1,505 practicing Christian adults, July 25–August 15, 2019.

Christians, 30% all others) say that all of the groups they've participated in began as part of an existing program through *some* kind of institution. However, compassionate and collaborative participants, by definition, have been a part of at least one group with more autonomous origins. More than one-quarter of practicing Christans who qualify as collaborative participants (27%) says their only experiences have been in original groups that did not spring from another program or institution.

In order to focus our learnings on people of faith who take such initiative, most of this report will be based on the responses of practicing Christians— self-identified Christians who attend church at least monthly and say their faith is very important in their lives—though comparisons will be drawn to other Christians and non-Christians where notable or instructive. As it stands, practicing Christians show a higher proportion of participants than those who aren't practicing Christians. Even of respondents who are community participants and not practicing Christians, 72 percent still self-identify as Christian. Most pastors surveyed for this study (89%) confirm that, in the past five years, their congregants have been part of groups which have gathered outside of church oversight to improve others' lives or pursue a passion or interest that benefited others. This is particularly true of ministries with more attendees and larger operating budgets or a great awareness of community needs. Nearly half of these groups (44%), pastors report, sprang up completely outside of church programs.

The existence of these groups supports the idea that people will find ways to improve their communities with or without religious institutions—but the prevalence of religious affiliation and church engagement among participants suggests faith may still be a present if not driving force for those pursuing the common good.

WHAT ARE GROUP FOUNDERS LIKE?

Barna categorized participants not only by their motivations and approach to engagement, but also by the role they say they have played within groups. Not surprisingly, simply being a member is the most common role. Six in 10 practicing Christian participants serve in this capacity. But who are those actually *starting* these groups?

Founders of groups with neighborhood impact are a rare minority—a group so small that the researchers can only examine their behavior among participants from the general population (of which they make up 9%). A plurality of founders (37%) are Millennials, making them both more likely than other roles to be students and less likely than other roles to be parents. Founders are also more likely to be representative of ethnic minorities.

This unique group of founders often live in urban areas (38%) and are highly likely to identify as Democrats (48%), demographic traits that usually correlate with being less religious. However, founders are more likely to be very committed to certain Christian beliefs and disciplines. Practicing Christian founders, more than other participants and even leaders of groups, feel responsible for sharing their faith, are convinced of scripture's accuracy, commonly volunteer at church and read the Bible regularly.

One area founders might need help: managing time and expectations. While most participants, even busy ones, don't struggle to find time to engage with a group, founders perhaps bear more of a burden. One in five (20% "completely true") says their experience within a group has made them too busy (vs. 5% of participants).

The Reach of Christians in Community

As mentioned previously in this chapter, all participants had to report being in groups with some sort of local effect in their city or town that reached beyond one's church. But, in an effort to learn from the varied forms that volunteerism or community engagement might take, the categories did not place other limits on where or to whom a group's work might reach. Encouragingly, practicing Christians engaged in groups offer a picture of a wide realm of influence, from personal to public and local to global. Open-ended responses underscored the diversity of activity, though many of the groups described had some focus on youth, whether through tutoring, sports, personal development or other services, or helping people affected by poverty.

Overall, three-quarters of practicing Christian participants (76%) say their community directly benefited because of a group they were involved in. Society in general (55%) and the disadvantaged in particular (53%) are also identified by the majority of participants as beneficiaries. About half say their churches or Christian communities were positively impacted.

There appears to be a boosted interest in and / or impact on environmental issues among those who are collaborative participants, with this group being most likely to say the natural world (32%) and animals (24%) saw some gain from their activities.

As far as *where* the groups had a general effect, responses reveal similar patterns of community or church impact. Collaborative participants are most likely to say their group involvement has risen to levels of national or global impact.

As the charts below detail, while group actions externally benefit others, those who are closely connected to the group may see personal benefit as well, hinting at a more holistic transformation for those who gather for the common good.

Who & Where: Beneficiaries of Groups

Base: practicing Christian community participants

TYPES OF PARTICIPANTS:
○ COMMUNITY ● COMPASSIONATE ● COLLABORATIVE

"Who benefited from this group?"

	Community	Compassionate	Collaborative
Our community	76%	78%	100%
People or society in general	55%	60%	64%
Disadvantaged people we felt compassion for	53%	59%	63%
A church / Christian community	50%	49%	52%
Group members	44%	45%	49%
Group members' loved ones	34%	34%	37%
The environment / natural world	23%	25%	32%
Something / someone else	17%	19%	23%
Another ideological, religious or faith community	16%	16%	21%
Animals	16%	19%	24%

"Where did your group have an effect?"

	Community	Compassionate	Collaborative
In our city or town	100%	100%	100%
In our church	57%	51%	56%
In our households	41%	42%	45%
In our country / nation or region of the world	34%	33%	40%
In another country / nation or region of the world	17%	15%	17%
All over the world / global	9%	12%	14%

n=392 U.S. practicing Christians who have been part of a group, July 25–August 15, 2019. Note that collaborative participants were required to identify their community as a beneficiary and all participants must have said their groups had an effect in their city or town.

Keys for Organizing & Measuring Neighborhood Actions

A Q&A WITH SHAWN DUNCAN, DONELL WOODSON & MONICA EVANS

Q: How can churches effectively equip their congregants to impact their community, even independently of the Church?

Shawn: I think this is an issue of formation, not about programming. We have disconnected discipleship from mission as if these are different departments and actions. We've divorced spirituality from mission as if these are different things. Churches ought to be forming the kind of people who live this way, not creating programs to manage it all.

I think a church could have resources and infrastructure to support these groups happening. They can and they should, but they're going to be much more

Dr. Shawn Duncan
is the director of the Lupton Center, the training and consulting division of Focused Community Strategies, a nonprofit community development organization in Atlanta.

Donell Woodson
is the lead trainer and consultant for community development at the Lupton Center.

Monica Evans
is the project manager for the Lupton Center.

decentralized. Instead of the church being the buffer between congregants and the community, the church says, "We're going to form and equip you to engage in your own unique context."

I think it's what we should be about, a sort of reversal of who's at the center. Is it a church's interest or God's activity in the world? Is it the congregation's campus or a neighborhood?

Q: What about the people who feel they have a calling to help those in need?

Monica: If you're walking into a place and you feel called to save these people, it's often because you don't know anything about them and you're making assumptions about them, assuming they need to be saved. If you're really going to be called to those people, go spend some time with them. Often, church posture is not to go be with people. Instead, it acts as a barrier between you and people, filtering everything that happens through a very tiny corridor of what the church says and believes.

Shawn: You may feel God calling you, but has the neighborhood called you? Have the people that you're concerned about voiced a call to you? You need both. I don't want to say that it's one or the other, but it's valuable to discern God's call in the context of a community confirming that they want you there. If you don't have that yet, then dial it back, take your time, build relationships and find out if your presence is even necessary.

Q: At the Lupton Center, you use specific tools and assessments to track the groups and people who are interacting with one another. Using these, how do you measure success? Is there anything groups should be aware of when it comes to these assessment tools?

Monica: In general, we sometimes think about success wrongly. If an organization or a program has been started and every year all they're thinking about is, "How many meals were served? How many kids were seen? How many vaccines were given?" then perhaps they're not asking, "What would it look like if we followed 30 families over the course of five years?" At Lupton Center, we encourage a more comprehensive, integrated system of tracking impact, something that allows us to know that the baby that we saw at five years old, who got their vaccines before they went to kindergarten, is now making good grades as a fifth grader. Often, we think about the people we're serving as just mouths to be fed or folks to be clothed for interviews as opposed to thinking about what it is that they need to help move them toward thriving. We need to reframe what success means.

Donell: We want to build the scale that Monica's talking about so we can say how many numbers we've reached. What we don't want is for the model itself to be built in such a way that the cycle of dependency continues.

What happens then is that people start to show up with expectancy. They may start to say, "I don't want what you're giving me. I actually want something else." Then the giver, who was at first finding gratification in being the hands and feet of Christ, might begin to think, "You should just take what I give. You are very ungrateful."

> "You're in an ecosystem in which large changes can be made if all the people who are doing their one tiny thing work together."

That paternalistic model creates a dependency on both sides. We often analyze this through the lens of the receiver, but it creates dependency for the giver as well, a sense of, "I need you to need me." That is something we don't want.

Q: With that measure of success in mind, what approach should community groups take when deciding where to work or who to serve?

Monica: I hear churches or people say, "We're just a tiny group doing this one thing." It's important to understand that you may be a small organization, but you're in an ecosystem in which large changes can be made if all the people who are doing their one tiny thing work together.

Think local. Draw a circle and ask, "Who are the people that I can be talking to in this place? How can we work together to make this place better?" I think large changes can happen if everybody is creating that loop and thinking about how to make the area better together.

Donell: Instead of the individual, the city or the larger 100-mile radius being the focus or central unit to thriving, we want to focus on the neighborhood. We're saying to the large or small parishes, the organization or the individual wanting to do good, you have a neighborhood, and place *matters*. It is key and essential.

Keys for Organizing & Measuring Neighborhood Actions

A Profile of Current Members

Much of this study asks respondents to reflect on groups they've been a part of at any point in their adulthood. We gain even greater clarity about the traits and environments that might nurture participation through a profile of *present* members of these communities. Indeed, 75 percent of practicing Christian community participants and 60 percent of all other participants say they are currently members of groups that meet to do something they are interested in and whose primary purpose is to benefit someone or something other than themselves. This stays relatively consistent across compassionate and collaborative participants as well. Looking at these individuals at the broadest level of engagement, there are few differences in demographic representation—even ones you might expect, such as generation, gender, education, parenting or income. Also, ethnically, there is no significant variation in either the practicing Christian sample or among those who are not practicing Christians.

In our total sample, singles are more likely than married adults to be participants (73% all single vs. 52% married), but this significant difference is not reflected among the practicing Christian respondents. Similarly, we see that, among community participants who aren't practicing Christians, single individuals with an income (typically Millennials with no kids) are more likely than married individuals with no income (typically Boomers and empty nesters) to commit to participation. Though, again, neither this nor any other difference around household or income type occurs among the sample of practicing Christians.

In many ways, these results refute our hypotheses. For instance, we assumed that those with lower or no level of employment, particularly empty nesters, might have more time to give to community engagement. Largely, this isn't the case. Similarly, you might think those who are married and have a dual income would have more resources to offer than other individuals, but this segment is also no more or less likely to be presently involved with a group. There is some correlation with parenting, though this relationship is also unexpected; parents and non-parents are just as likely to be present participants, and, in fact, those parenting children through the seemingly very hands-on age range of 6–12-years-old are *more* likely than those with grown children to be in a group at this time.

Barna decided to cut to the heart of our query and test whether a certain level of busyness might prevent people from investing in a community group. Researchers developed a scale of busyness, based on respondents' reports of weekly hours spent on paid *and* unpaid work. On this point too, whether one is very busy (70+ hours accounted for), moderately busy (40–69 hours) or not so busy (less than 40 hours), it has no significant impact on the likelihood that one is currently taking steps to contribute to one's local community. Among practicing Christians, about three-quarters of each of these groups is a present participant.

So, what are the common denominators, if not these traits?

Sharing Means Caring: Common Ground Among Members

Barna was able to identify some areas in which it seems important for members of groups to overlap and relate. The main one? Passion.

Let's Talk About: CONNECTION POINTS FOR COMMUNITY PARTICIPANTS

"We have found just as many conservative-leaning, older white people whose lives have really been guided in this really profound, redemptive direction as younger, minority, liberal-guided people. Both are capable of participating in this redemptive work."
–Dr. Shawn Duncan, Lupton Center

"Many people in our culture wonder if the Church will survive. I think the way forward is for us to begin to think more carefully about how we join with others and serve them through three areas of calling: at work, at home and in the community."
–Glenn Barth, Good Cities

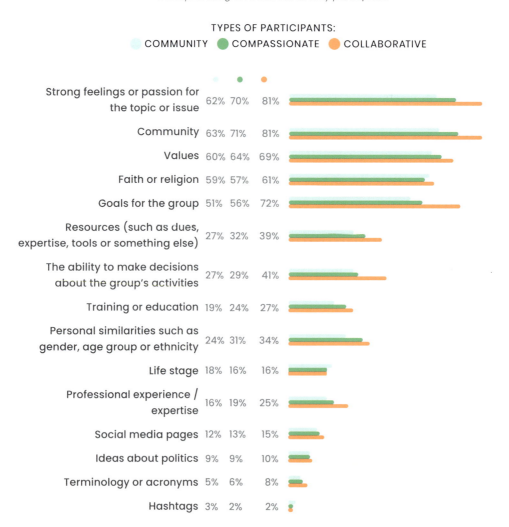

Data show that participants in groups with neighborhood impact often share passions for causes, as well as values and community—even more so than they share their faith or religion specifically. This pattern holds steady even when we restrict the sample to practicing Christians alone, underscoring both the unifying quality of these cause-oriented groups as well as the possibility that these Christians are extending themselves beyond organized church or programs. By comparison, participants are less often akin to one another in demographic characteristics like life stage, gender, age, ethnicity or political ideology. This finding is even more remarkable when we consider other Barna studies that show people tend to gather only with friends of mostly similar backgrounds and beliefs[7] and often struggle to talk across divides.[8] It raises a question—and a solution: Could an intentional, generous level of local engagement create unique opportunities for connection, in spite of our homogeneous communities and increasingly polarized culture? (*See page 65 to learn more about how diversity can be a sign of a strong community of action.*)

Shared passions for a cause or topic are more common among the compassionate (70%) and collaborative (81%) participants for whom it is part of the definition, but even among practicing Christians who are general community participants, 62 percent say that a passion

> Participants in groups with neighborhood impact often share passions for causes, as well as values and community—even more so than they share their faith or religion specifically

Let's Talk About: CONNECTION POINTS FOR COMMUNITY PARTICIPANTS

"That was the common denominator. They all had a heart for community engagement."
–Lynn Heatley, *Love Riverside*

"I think people just want to be known, but they want to be known for who they are, not who you say they are."
–Kitti Murray, *Refuge Coffee Co.*

"Typically, a group starts with a person or people grabbing a vision and passion for something. Then, they either find people who have like-minded passions or pull that passion out of others who connect with it immediately when given the opportunity."
–Stephanie Wieber, *Palau Association*

A Spectrum of Engagement

Get to know the one in four practicing Christians who have gathered with others and taken initiative in their neighborhoods.

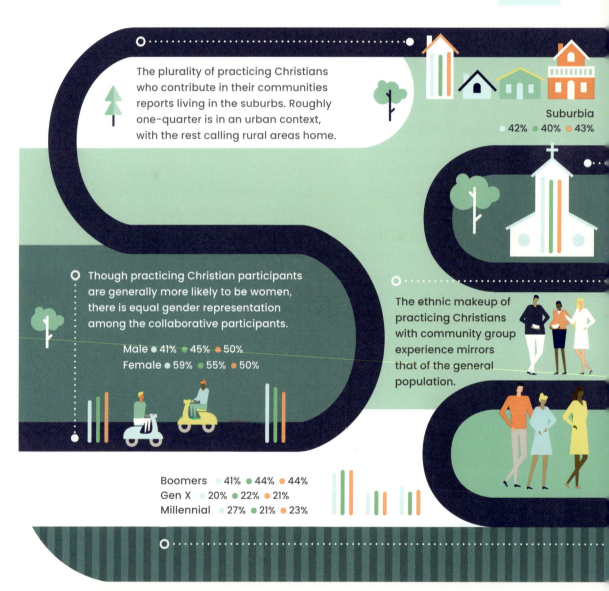

The plurality of practicing Christians who contribute in their communities reports living in the suburbs. Roughly one-quarter is in an urban context, with the rest calling rural areas home.

Suburbia ● 42% ● 40% ● 43%

Though practicing Christian participants are generally more likely to be women, there is equal gender representation among the collaborative participants.

Male ● 41% ● 45% ● 50%
Female ● 59% ● 55% ● 50%

The ethnic makeup of practicing Christians with community group experience mirrors that of the general population.

Boomers ● 41% ● 44% ● 44%
Gen X ● 20% ● 22% ● 21%
Millennial ● 27% ● 21% ● 23%

n=392 U.S. practicing Christians who were part of a group (including 176 practicing Christians who were compassionate participants and 118 practicing Christians who were collaborative participants), July 25–August 19, 2019.

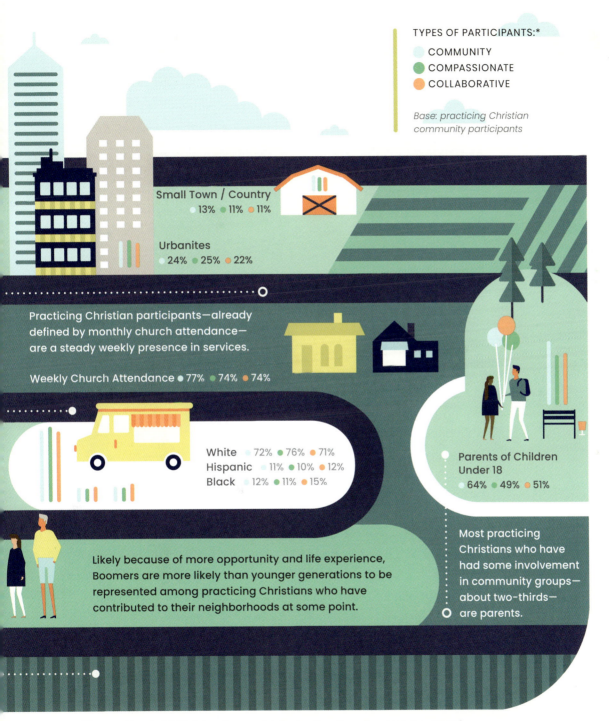

TYPES OF PARTICIPANTS:*
- COMMUNITY
- COMPASSIONATE
- COLLABORATIVE

Base: practicing Christian community participants

Small Town / Country
● 13% ● 11% ● 11%

Urbanites
● 24% ● 25% ● 22%

Practicing Christian participants—already defined by monthly church attendance—are a steady weekly presence in services.

Weekly Church Attendance ● 77% ● 74% ● 74%

White   ● 72% ● 76% ● 71%
Hispanic ● 11% ● 10% ● 12%
Black   ● 12% ● 11% ● 15%

Parents of Children Under 18
● 64% ● 49% ● 51%

Likely because of more opportunity and life experience, Boomers are more likely than younger generations to be represented among practicing Christians who have contributed to their neighborhoods at some point.

Most practicing Christians who have had some involvement in community groups—about two-thirds—are parents.

*See page 14 or the Methodology for more details about how these groupings were created.

A Spectrum of Engagement

> Vocational or entrepreneurial networks may be fertile ground for encouraging individuals toward neighborhood influence

for a specific issue was the common ground on which they gathered. Similar proportions of community participants indicate they rallied around their shared values (60%) or communities (63%). Again, we should expect to see more in common among the narrow categories of participation, whose identity somewhat hinges on these factors. Still, it's worth noting that a majority of practicing Christian participants with compassionate (54%) and collaborative (71%) engagement identifies at least five things shared among members of their groups.

One interesting quality observed in participants with collaborative experiences is a greater likelihood of sharing professional backgrounds (25% collaborative vs. 19% compassionate, 16% community). Similar training or education is also more common as you move through the funnel of participation (19% community, 24% compassionate, 27% collaborative). It's possible that vocational or entrepreneurial networks may be fertile ground for encouraging individuals toward neighborhood influence or fostering greater levels of concern, initiative and involvement.

Affective Learning: How Congregants Move from Passion to Action

BY REV. DR. JASON BROGE

As you look at your congregation, what are your hopes for the people you see as they grow closer to the Lord? For example, do you want them to be people who only *know about* prayer? Or do you want them to be people who *enjoy the experience* of prayer? Maybe even people who *affirm the value* of prayer? People who *turn to prayer naturally* in all situations, never ceasing, joyfully making all requests known to God?

In this same way, consider the positive impact you hope they will make on their neighborhoods. As you prepare sermons and Bible studies on the Good Samaritan, what effect do you hope it will have on the people in your congregation? Would you be satisfied if they acknowledged hurt and harm happening to their neighbor? Or would you want them to go beyond that to actually help and support their neighbor in every physical need?[9]

As leaders, we want more for people. We want to help them move from care to action. This developmental shift is important. This report shows that the vast majority of people who come together with members of the neighborhood and have a positive impact shares "strong feelings or passion"

Rev. Dr. Jason Broge

is director of design and development for global ministries at Lutheran Hour Ministries. Broge served as a teacher for a number of years before becoming a pastor. After obtaining his PhD in education, he went on to serve as the director of curriculum design and development for Concordia Seminary.

about the issue they are trying to impact. As a leader in the church, you likely know people who say they have strong passions and yet they do nothing with these said feelings. How do we help people move from care to action? How do we nurture passion to the point where people cannot help but run to get involved?

This question has plagued church leaders for hundreds of years. I can still hear my pastoral supervisor bemoaning the lack of action on the congregation's part during my pastoral internship. "What do they want from me? Why won't they show up to help?" It seems as though it should be a fairly simple thing. If we just teach about the biblical mandate for Christians to love their neighbor, if we just explain how we as Christians in America today can "help and support" our neighbor in "every physical need," they will go and do likewise … right? Too often, they don't. So, how do you help people move from care to action?

Educational theory can help us here. Educators recognize the difference between "cognitive" (knowledge-based) learning, skills-based learning and "affective" (value-based) learning. They have sought for decades to find ways to influence not just what a student knows and does but what motivates them to the point of putting that knowledge and skill into action.[10] The affective domain describes learning in this area as going through a series of stages. These stages can be described as a process whereby the learner moves from being unaware of the existence of something to having a deeply felt internalized value that characterizes their behaviors naturally.

Key for educators is creating experiences that allow learners to not just learn facts but to go through this affective process from one stage to the next. One can spend a lifetime exploring this, but as you look for ways to apply this to your congregation it is helpful to ask a few basic questions.

- **Where has God gifted my congregation with passion and abilities already?** Often, as ministry leaders, we want to begin with causes we personally are passionate about or actions we are gifted in. But if the congregation doesn't share our passions or giftedness, the efforts will inevitably be more difficult. It will require you to not only teach skills and knowledge but also create the passion to fuel it. Sometimes this might be what you're called to do—but sometimes it might mean your pet projects or passions are perhaps not truly representative of the strengths of your congregation or the needs of the neighborhood. If you have people who are passionate about education or poverty or adoption in your congregation, chances are this isn't an accident. If your congregation is full of car mechanics and nurses, chances are this isn't an accident. God has gifted your congregation with those passions and gifts, which might make them the perfect places to start reaching out into the local community.

- **How can we create opportunities for service that provide satisfaction for the learner?** It is not uncommon for ministry leaders to be suspicious of opportunities where the servant seems to get more out of the experience than those who are being served. If this is the only service you find in your congregation, then I can see why that may be concerning—but there is still an important place for service experiences that are rewarding. Finding satisfaction in an experience is an important stage in affective learning. This means considering the impact of a service project on those who are serving is important too.

- **How can we create opportunities for people to create opportunities?** We do not want disciples who are only interested in loving their neighbor when they are in our church buildings. We hope for people who are, and indeed pray we ourselves would become, followers of Christ characterized by a love for God and love for neighbor in every aspect of our lives. If we want people to take this into their neighborhoods, then we need to give them the space to imagine possibilities outside the scope of congregational ministry. They need to see their calling not from or to the Church, but from God to the people in the world around them.

It is possible to help people move from only caring about their neighborhood to actually doing more for their neighborhood. But it requires us as church leaders to examine our goals and be open to creating new opportunities for people to move through the stages of affective learning. If your goal is to have people value prayer, you will have to create opportunities for them to have enjoyable prayer experiences. If your goal is to have people value acts of service, you will need to create opportunities where the servers find a sense of satisfaction from the experience of service.

If, on the other hand, your goal is to have someone deepen their values, you must create opportunities for them to be able to choose things on their own in light of that value. If your goal is to deepen a value for prayer, then you should create opportunities and an environment where people can initiate prayer on their own. If your goal is to deepen a value for service, then you should create opportunities and an environment where people can initiate service on their own, in their own neighborhoods. Throughout this process, you as a church leader will constantly be juggling the need to dictate and direct with the need to resource and empower based on where people are in their affective journey.

Why Community Groups Act:

THE INTERESTS & ISSUES THAT PROMPT CHRISTIANS TO ORGANIZE

Psychologists David Desteno and Piercarlo Valdesolo once conducted an experiment in which subjects—who were total strangers—were more likely to identify with and help one another throughout a series of tests if they first spent time tapping their hands in unison.[11] Their conclusion: something about synchronicity can evoke camaraderie and altruism. If something as simple as a little mindless choreography fosters a sense of teamwork and compassion, how much might more intentional or heartfelt shared efforts bind us together and inspire us toward good works?

In this chapter, we'll explore a series of survey questions that speak to the underlying interests that inspire action groups and their members.

Reasons for Gathering

Barna asked participants to select reasons that their groups came together, and the top motivation for practicing Christians is generous:

> The top motivation for practicing Christian participants is generous: to help others

to help others (68%). Celebration or worship also surfaces as a primary reason that members come together, which sets practicing Christians apart; they are significantly more likely than participants who are not practicing Christians (60% vs. 34%) to select this spiritual driver for participation. Other common reasons for gathering are more relational or recreational, like connecting over things they like or are interested in in order to develop friendships.

Percentages climb for most motivations as you look across the spectrum of participants. Compassionate and collaborative participants are more drawn to or emphatic about almost every reason for gathering. More than half of collaborative participants (53%)—who, as we've noted, often share professional backgrounds or interests with their fellow members—say their groups formed to create or build something, which could reflect entrepreneurial instincts.

Filtered by ethnicity, black practicing Christians are significantly more likely than white practicing Christians to be in groups that aim to produce change (65% vs. 35%) and dialogue (54% vs. 36%) or to build something new (48% vs. 32%).

Generationally, Boomers are more likely than Millennials to clearly be looking for opportunities to help others (75% vs. 55%) through group participation. Millennials gather around other signs of curiosity,

Let's Talk About: MOTIVATIONS FOR ACTION

"If you don't love your city, you're not going to have the right motive in serving it."
–Lynn Heatley, Love Riverside

"Every community has different places where they feel a lack of flourishing. We feel like the local church will be the biggest blessing to the community if they are able to engage with the things that the specific community says are challenges."
–Ruth Evans, Unite

like a desire to have fun (62% vs. 37% of Boomers), learn something new (58% vs. 34%) or connect with others over things they like (52% vs. 39%). Still, this innovating younger generation sees their groups as avenues to create (47% vs. 27%) or change something (46% vs. 31%).

Of course, a *group's* reasons for forming or gathering could be quite different than an *individual's* reasons for joining said group. Yet even on the personal level, motivations are relatively the same: a mix

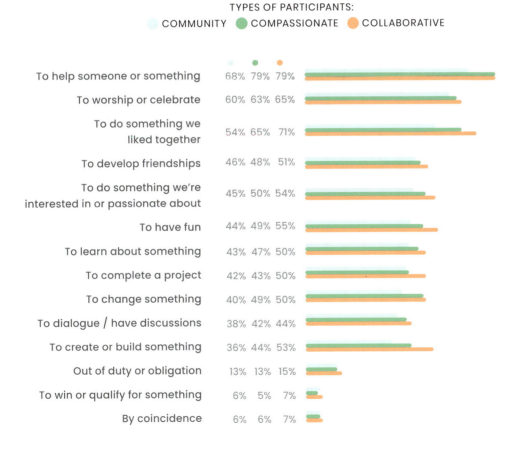

Group Reasons for Gathering
Base: practicing Christian community participants

TYPES OF PARTICIPANTS:
COMMUNITY • COMPASSIONATE • COLLABORATIVE

	Community	Compassionate	Collaborative
To help someone or something	68%	79%	79%
To worship or celebrate	60%	63%	65%
To do something we liked together	54%	65%	71%
To develop friendships	46%	48%	51%
To do something we're interested in or passionate about	45%	50%	54%
To have fun	44%	49%	55%
To learn about something	43%	47%	50%
To complete a project	42%	43%	50%
To change something	40%	49%	50%
To dialogue / have discussions	38%	42%	44%
To create or build something	36%	44%	53%
Out of duty or obligation	13%	13%	15%
To win or qualify for something	6%	5%	7%
By coincidence	6%	6%	7%

n=392 U.S. practicing Christian adults who were part of a group, July 25–August 15, 2019.

of social, spiritual and charitable inclinations, bolstered by shared interests. Here, too, many catalysts for involvement become even more of a factor as participants shift toward the compassionate and then collaborative end of the spectrum. These two segments are aligned in primarily being driven to do good (67% and 69%, respectively). (Note these are motivations reported for participation in the group that respondents considered to be most successful.)

Personal Reasons for Being Involved in a Group

Base: practicing Christian community participants

TYPES OF PARTICIPANTS:
COMMUNITY • COMPASSIONATE • COLLABORATIVE

Reason	Community	Compassionate	Collaborative
Faith / religious beliefs	61%	54%	58%
Doing good	59%	67%	69%
Desire for community / friends	47%	48%	53%
Personal passion	46%	43%	48%
Helping people help themselves	43%	50%	54%
Biblical instruction	30%	27%	35%
A personal experience of the need	24%	23%	29%
Promoting social justice	17%	22%	22%
Wanting to support someone else involved in the group	16%	21%	25%
Love of nature / the outdoors	12%	20%	25%
Promoting equality	11%	15%	19%
Love of animals	8%	12%	13%
Patriotism	8%	9%	12%
Something else	7%	9%	10%

n=205 U.S. practicing Christian adults who were part of a group, July 25–August 15, 2019. When answering this question, participants were asked to think about the most successful group they'd been a part of.

We're focused on practicing Christians here, who differ significantly from those who are not practicing Christians when it comes to personal reasons for joining. Expectedly, for the latter, factors like faith (24% vs. 61% of all practicing Christian participants) and biblical instruction (7% vs. 30%) diminish significantly in influence, but a longing for community (65% vs. 47%) or to "help others help themselves" (53% vs. 43%) become stronger drivers for group participation. For these participants who aren't practicing Christians, about one in four gets involved simply as a show of solidarity, to support another member (26% vs. 16%).

Personal passion (56% Millennials vs. 36% Boomers) but also biblical instruction (44% vs. 25%) provide momentum for practicing Christian Millennials more so than for Boomers. Given younger adults' reputation for being less religious, church leaders might be encouraged that, at least among faithful Millennials, scripture seems to be driving this behavior. It's possible they credit such convictions for their deeper personal interest in promoting equality (21% vs. 6%) through action groups.

To analyze this range of reasons from another angle, Barna grouped the drivers for participation as either internal or external motivations—internal being emotional, inward motivations that might

> Personal passion but also biblical instruction provide momentum for Millennials

Let's Talk About: MOTIVATIONS FOR ACTION

"Communities of action meet some need or an intersection of needs that can't be otherwise met, a place where a way has not yet been found to integrate these two narratives."
–Scott Kauffman, Praxis

"People who discovered mission or action as a core part of their Christian identity and sustained it over many years as a part of their lifestyle were those that had entered into mutual relationship with the people they served."
–Dr. Shawn Duncan, Lupton Center

center around personal interests or principles (*desire for community / friends, love of nature / the outdoors, personal experience of the need, love of animals, biblical instruction, personal passion, faith / religious beliefs*) and external being outward motivations that might center around the context or well-being of others (*social justice, equality, helping people help themselves, patriotism, supporting someone else involved in the group*). Though we ultimately can't speak to the deeply personal nature of these beliefs or convictions, and their impact may be both private and public, these two categories do allow us to loosely organize and observe them.

Internal motivations (96%) are far more common than external ones (61%). For most practicing Christians, the internal and external naturally overlap—of those who were externally motivated to join a group that benefited the community, more than nine of 10 (94%) are also internally motivated, and of those who are internally motivated, about three of five (60%) are also externally motivated. Four in 10 participants (39%), however, are *only* driven by internal reasons for involvement (usually faith or friendship).

Members who qualify as compassionate (73%) or collaborative (79%) are significantly more likely to claim external motivations for their personal participation, which may have to do with these groups' core emphasis on facilitating change or providing help to their communities.

The Power of Passion

62% of practicing Christians who participated in a community group shared a strong passion for the cause with their fellow group members. In several dimensions, this mutual enthusiasm correlates with deeper engagement and positive outcomes.

● COMMUNITY PARTICIPANTS IN GROUPS THAT SHARE A PASSION
● COMMUNITY PARTICIPANTS IN GROUPS THAT DO NOT SHARE A PASSION

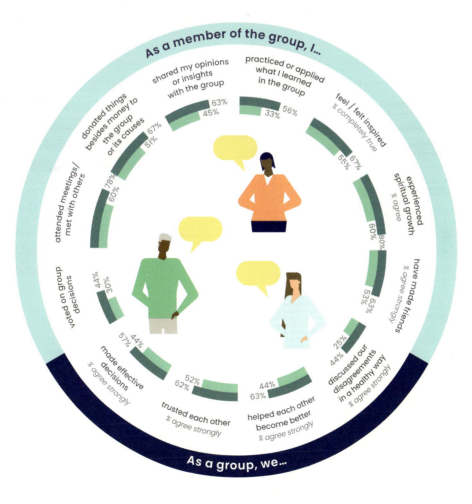

As a member of the group, I…
- shared my opinions or insights with the group: 63% / 45%
- practiced or applied what I learned in the group: 56% / 33%
- feel / felt inspired (% completely true): 67% / 55%
- experienced spiritual growth (% agree): 80% / 60%
- have made friends (% agree strongly): 63% / 53%
- discussed our disagreements in a healthy way (% agree strongly): 44% / 25%
- donated things besides money to the group or its causes: 67% / 51%
- attended meetings / met with others: 78% / 60%
- voted on group decisions: 44% / 30%

As a group, we…
- made effective decisions (% agree strongly): 57% / 44%
- trusted each other (% agree strongly): 62% / 52%
- helped each other become better (% agree strongly): 63% / 44%

n=392 U.S. practicing Christians who were part of a group, July 25–August 19, 2019. Participants were asked to think about the most successful group they'd been a part of.

Serving Neighborhoods Through Creativity

A Q&A WITH MAKOTO FUJIMURA

Q: Some would say that art is a skillset that perhaps doesn't have a natural place in service toward others. How would you combat that statement? How can creative individuals use their skillsets serve others or enact change within a community?

A: Art is more than a "skillset" in that it moves beyond the utilitarian. The reason why this is important, as Lewis Hyde notes in his seminal work *The Gift,* is because art moves beyond the industrial utility, and therefore captures the most important essence of humanity. In other words, art captures what is human, beyond our role as mechanistic, or part of a closed mechanism of nature, into the transcendent future.

Q: Have you yourself been a part of or seen a community group form in which the participants used art or other creative skillsets to serve their neighborhood? What were some of the challenges they faced? What were some of the outcomes from this group's action, whether positive or negative?

A: My church, All Saints Church in Princeton, dedicated the entire fall season to culture care based on my book *Culture Care*. It was a remarkable fall, from empowering congregants to see themselves as artists of the Kingdom to having a choir director combine Jewish congregation singers with the All Saints choir. The challenge is always to make sure everyone sees themselves as part of culture care, whether they are an artist or not.

Q: Data show that pastors believe that churches with lay-led initiatives are healthier than those without, however, pastors often feel inadequate when it comes to empowering the leaders of these initiatives. How can churches specifically make space for and empower creative individuals to serve others?

A: Artists can be essential leaders to the Church, as they are, in Dr. Howard Gardner's words from *Multiple Intelligences,* "in the enterprise of persuasion" and therefore key leaders. My next book, *Theology of Making,* outlines how making or creating is central to theology, which therefore designates artists as key elements of church growth.

> "Making or creating is central to theology, which therefore designates artists as key elements of church growth."

Makoto Fujimura is an artist, writer and speaker who is recognized worldwide as a cultural shaper. A presidential appointee to the National Council on the Arts from 2003–2009, Fujimura served as an international advocate for the arts, speaking with decision makers and advising governmental policies on the arts. In 2014, the American Academy of Religion named Fujimura as its Religion and the Arts award recipient. He has had numerous exhibits at museums including Tikotin Museum in Israel and Gonzaga Jundt Museum. New York's Waterfall Mansion & Gallery and Asia's Artrue Gallery represent his works. *New York Times* columnist David Brooks recently featured Fujimura's work and described his book *Culture Care* as "a small rebellion against the quickening of time."

Causes & Concerns

"Are there any particular causes or issues which might affect your local community that you are particularly passionate or concerned about? Select all."

Base: practicing Christian community participants

TYPES OF PARTICIPANTS:
● COMMUNITY ● COMPASSIONATE ● COLLABORATIVE

	Community	Compassionate	Collaborative
Local poverty	50%	54%	57%
Strengthening families	49%	46%	46%
Child protection	40%	42%	46%
Special needs (physical or mental)	39%	45%	45%
Medical services	29%	33%	38%
Access to education for children	28%	26%	24%
Environmental issues	27%	27%	31%
Strengthening marriages	27%	25%	30%
Caring for orphans and foster children	24%	25%	28%
Economic development through small businesses	19%	23%	27%
Medical research on diseases	17%	19%	23%
Political activism	15%	15%	15%
Refugee response	11%	13%	15%
Other	6%	4%	3%
None of these	5%	5%	5%

n=232 U.S. practicing Christian adults who were part of a group, July 25–August 15, 2019.

Causes That Participants Care About

If passion is so paramount to those who gather within and for their communities, what are they passionate about?

When asked to think about causes or issues that have some impact on their local community, fighting poverty and strengthening families emerge as the central concerns for practicing Christians who have had some group involvement. Other commonly chosen causes focus on vulnerable communities, such as children or those with special needs. Issues that could be considered politically charged, like activism, refugee response and economic development, appear lower on the list. The three participant types follow similar patterns when it comes to their priorities.

These are the passions and causes that tug on heartstrings, pique interest, inspire creativity or stir convictions to the point that Christians are prompted to find others who feel the same. In the following chapter, we'll probe further: What are the dynamics and outcomes of those affinity groups?

The Logistics of Gathering in & Impacting Community

This report has covered *why* lay-led groups begin, but it's also important to understand *how* they function. In this section, we'll let respondents describe the habits and organization of the most successful communities they've been a part of. To better provide insights on foundations of all thriving groups and keys for churches wanting to practically support them, we won't single out practicing Christians here but will instead learn from community-minded participants both inside and outside the Church. However, due to the research methodology, note that this sample does favor practicing Christians, who represent 75 percent of total respondents.

HOW THEY GATHER

Naturally, meetings are a regular part of participating in any group. As a baseline qualification in this study, participants indicated they had been in a group that gathered at least three times, but the majority

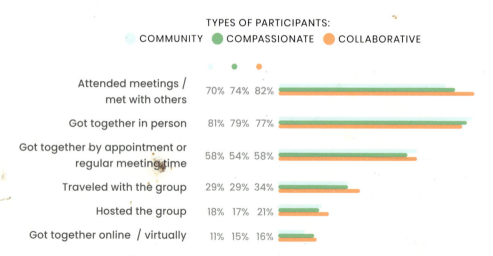

Group Meetings

TYPES OF PARTICIPANTS:
● COMMUNITY ● COMPASSIONATE ● COLLABORATIVE

	Community	Compassionate	Collaborative
Attended meetings / met with others	70%	74%	82%
Got together in person	81%	79%	77%
Got together by appointment or regular meeting time	58%	54%	58%
Traveled with the group	29%	29%	34%
Hosted the group	18%	17%	21%
Got together online / virtually	11%	15%	16%

n=274 U.S. adults who were part of a group, July 25–August 15, 2019. When answering this question, participants were asked to think about the most successful group they'd been a part of.

of members also specifies that regularly meeting with others is part of participation in a successful association. About one-fifth mentions actually hosting the group. Usually, meetings require an appointment or standing scheduled time and don't happen off-the-cuff. In-person gatherings are the norm, though one in 10 meets virtually. Some groups, about one-third, go so far as traveling together.

Usually these groups start as strangers; more than half (54%) say nobody knew each other before joining. More than one-quarter (28%) says most of them were already friends, while one in five (18%) says there was someone in the group who knew everyone else and brought them together.

HOW THEY ARE FUNDED

Few participants, about one in 10, have engaged with groups that had no expenses. The primary method of funding activities is through donations, though more than one-third says members pay dues. Indeed, half

Group Finances

TYPES OF PARTICIPANTS:
COMMUNITY COMPASSIONATE COLLABORATIVE

	COMMUNITY	COMPASSIONATE	COLLABORATIVE
Donations	69%	70%	71%
Dues / everyone chipped in	36%	35%	37%
Payment for goods or services the group provided	19%	20%	25%
The purpose of our group was to raise money	19%	17%	20%
Grants	14%	19%	24%
Another organization covered expenses	12%	10%	12%
There were no expenses	10%	8%	7%
Loans	2%	1%	2%
Other	5%	5%	7%

n=274 U.S. adults who were part of a group, July 25–August 15, 2019. When answering this question, participants were asked to think about the most successful group they'd been a part of.

of participants say they have given money to a group or its causes. Some initiatives have other ways of self-sustaining; about one in five says the very purpose of a group is raising funds, similar to the proportion who says a group sells goods or services to cover expenses. Sizable minorities of community groups operate like many charities or non-profits, receiving grants, loans or support from other organizations.

HOW PARTICIPANTS ENGAGE

Beyond financial donations, non-monetary contributions are also quite common. Six in 10 participants report giving something other than money to a group or its cause. Other members lend knowledge or expertise, with a majority sharing opinions with the group and more than one-third providing actual teaching or coaching. About four in 10 also exercise their voice in helping make group

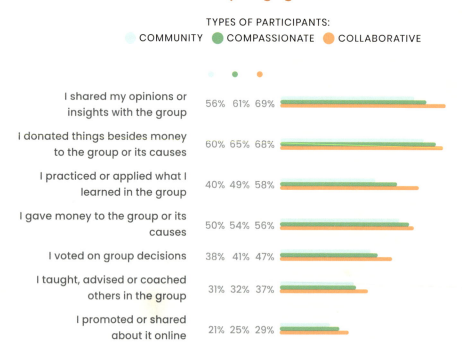

Group Engagement

TYPES OF PARTICIPANTS:
● COMMUNITY ● COMPASSIONATE ● COLLABORATIVE

	Community	Compassionate	Collaborative
I shared my opinions or insights with the group	56%	61%	69%
I donated things besides money to the group or its causes	60%	65%	68%
I practiced or applied what I learned in the group	40%	49%	58%
I gave money to the group or its causes	50%	54%	56%
I voted on group decisions	38%	41%	47%
I taught, advised or coached others in the group	31%	32%	37%
I promoted or shared about it online	21%	25%	29%

n=528 U.S. adults who were part of a group, July 25–August 15, 2019.

decisions. Across the group spectrum, about one-fifth is posting online about their group as well. Members aren't just contributing, but also receiving; as many as 58 percent of collaborative participants say they practice or apply things they've learned from the group.

The Value of Local Learning & Listening

A Q&A WITH GREG RUSSINGER

Q: How did you invite or gather people to become involved with Laundry Love, a non-profit that washes the bedding and clothes of low / no income families?

A: For the first few years, there was only one Laundry Love location. Then, over time, an organic interest began to rise about Laundry Love and more locations were added as people began to learn what we were doing. I think Laundry Love helped answer the question, "What can we do in our neighborhood, city and town?" So we coached and guided people and groups in the early days of the movement.

More churches got wind of Laundry Love, then neighbors learned about it and wanted to start one, and then non-faith groups and diverse faith groups. We connected with so many groups who saw this as a simple human care initiative that comes alongside the low- to no-income families and individuals in their area. Laundry Love is about people joining together. It's about dignity. People said yes.

Q: What do you think contributed to the success of Laundry Love?

A: In short, its simplicity. It was an open source idea. And you have nothing but time in a laundromat, and what we've learned is people still enjoy the face-to-face interaction, the connection and the shared experience.

Laundry Love believes in meaningful collaboration, and so we encourage every location to seek interagency alliances and partnerships. Whether it be job placement agencies, housing placement agencies, food or clothing options, tutoring children or providing basic medical options, there are so many different ways community and city alliances help in a holistic way.

Laundry Love can be contextualized for every neighborhood and city. Laundry Love is not a project or an event, it's a relational commitment. Laundry Love is about returning. Returning is a practice of love. God in his grace returns to us, his creation, time and time again. The Samaritan story is a great example of this. In bringing the man to an inn, the next day the Samaritan gives the inn keeper some money and says "Look after him" and *when I return.* " Human care requires consistency. Laundry Love fosters this awareness in those who serve so that they soon realize this not something "we" do for "them," but this is an "us" thing. It's an expression of living *with*. It's solidarity. It's mutuality. It's love.

We tell people to enter laundromats not only to make a difference, but so those you serve make you different.

family needs. If the good news is the good news, then we have to be a listening people who ask really good questions. What is good news to this family, this city, this person? Start there (as Jesus did in Matthew 20:32; Mark 10:51 and Luke 18:41).

I don't think we can fully experience what the kingdom life is about if we're not engaging. Yes, the Church should empower, get involved and support. All of it.

Q: In what way should the church try to empower their members to start or lead ministries like this? Do you think churches should get involved with lay-led ministries or is it better for them to support the ministry in another way?

A: I think one practice is to listen well. Don't make assumptions for your community. You have to be out in the community and listen to what's really happening. Listening is absolutely essential for there to be any sort of healthy and longstanding engagement. There can be a tendency for a church to assume what a neighborhood, a city or even a

Greg Russinger

Father to Ashtin and Liam, husband to Michele, Russinger is co-founder and board president of Laundry Love, pastor at Alongsiders Church in Portland, Oregon, an author, speaker, musician, consultant, film lover and staunch soccer player / fan. Follow him at @gregrussinger @laundrylove

What Community Groups Achieve:
AN OVERVIEW OF DYNAMICS & OUTCOMES

This study alone can't quantify the actual success of certain groups—not without having great detail about what they did and how they operated, as well as community reports about how they were received. Further, metrics of success vary depending upon the unique purposes and contexts of groups—and likely upon whom you ask! Ultimately, perhaps only the neighborhoods in which groups gather, influence and act should determine their effectiveness. For the aims of this study, however, we'll isolate several self-reported outcomes (both personal and public) that, on their surface, could be seen as positive and see if we can learn how to nurture these results.

As Barna set out to discover what makes a group effective toward its goals and in its neighborhood, we asked participants to keep their most successful group in mind during a specific portion of the survey. We wanted to learn what goes into these favored groups—their characteristics, organization, engagement and emotional climates—and what might keep participants involved for the long haul. The data show there are strong correlations between participation and things like spiritual growth, positive emotional responses, deeper community and new perspectives. Changing in these ways not only benefits an individual, but in turn may also flow out into the community, in a giving cycle.

In this chapter, we won't focus much on compassionate and collaborative participants, but on all community participants, as there are actually very few significant differences among them when it comes to results and outcomes. This in itself, however, is worth noting: While the participant categories are helpful for identifying different types of participants and groups and the drivers of their involvement, in many cases, it appears individuals can begin at any point and arrive at impact, companionship or spiritual growth.

Group Experiences

Let's start with the overall personal and collective experiences that practicing Christian participants have in the groups they consider to be "most successful."

A majority says that being a part of such a group contributes to feelings of happiness (73% completely true) and inspiration (63% completely true). Spiritual development also often accompanies practicing Christians' involvement; more than half (53%) strongly agree the experience has deepened their relationship with God. Other personal changes—such as a changed mind, for instance—are less common for these practicing Christians; one in five (20% completely true) says some evolution of thought occurred because of what they learned in the group, though a greater proportion (28% not true at all) says this hasn't been their experience at all.

Whether or not members teach one another or change minds, participants largely indicate that successful groups have positive social environments. Most—six in 10—feel they have made new friends (60% strongly agree) and that group members trust one another (59% strongly agree) and make each other better (57% strongly agree). They recall constructive exchanges where people hold a variety of ideas

> Spiritual development often accompanies practicing Christians' group involvement

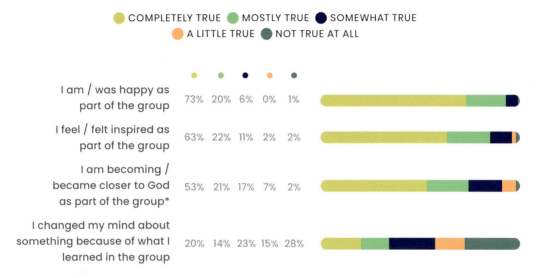

n=205 U.S. practicing Christian adults who were part of a group, July 25–August 15, 2019. When answering this question, participants were asked to think about the most successful group they'd been a part of. *For this response, the scale was: strongly agree, somewhat agree, neither agree nor disagree, somewhat disagree, strongly disagree.

(42% strongly agree), even opposing ones, but manage to communicate them in healthy ways (37% strongly agree). Accordingly, very few say that, in successful group contexts, a bully is or was present (73% strongly disagree). It's worth noting that, though some become involved in groups *specifically* to make friends, data show that those who gather to make a difference are just as likely to make friends from involvement in a successful group.

With this positive assessment of group culture in mind, it's perhaps no surprise that participants see good organization (57% strongly

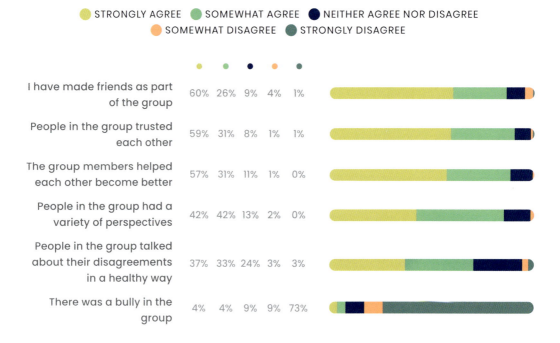

agree) in successful groups. More than half (52% strongly agree) also point to a smooth decision-making process. And though this might be a reflection of their own commitment level as much as the time management or expectations of the group, most say their involvement did not make their personal schedule become too busy (57% not true at all).

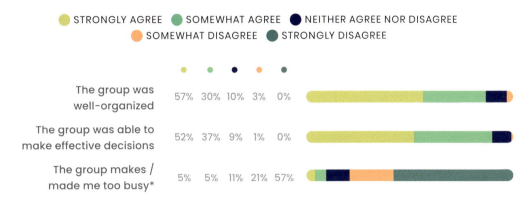

n=205 U.S. practicing Christian adults who were part of a group, July 25–August 15, 2019. When answering this question, participants were asked to think about the most successful group they'd been a part of. *For this response, the scale was: completely true, mostly true, somewhat true, a little true, not true at all.*

THE LAGGING ENGAGEMENT OF BOOMERS

Boomers' experiences within even successful community groups raise some cause for concern. Across many of the results you'd hope to see from positive engagement with a neighborhood, older practicing Christians' reports trail their younger peers. Boomers are less likely to say their involvement in such a group led them to make friends (81% vs. 94% of Millennials somewhat + strongly agree), grow spiritually (69% vs. 78% of Millennials and 78% of Gen X somewhat + strongly agree), feel inspired (58% vs. 70% Millennials and 78% Gen X say it's completely true) or change their mind about something (24% vs. 48% Millennials and 57% Gen X say it's mostly + completely true). Interestingly, though Boomers still indicate there was a strong degree of trust among the group members, they are less likely to say disagreements were handled in healthy ways (29% vs. 52% of Millennials and 52% of Gen X strongly agree).

It should be considered that some Millennials and Gen X practicing Christians could be, in hindsight, inclined to give reviews that are more glowing than the reality of their time with a group. But it may be that Boomers' returns on participation simply reflect their lesser emotional investment; for instance, personal passions are rarely a reason they join a group (36%), while this is a common driver for younger adults (56% Millennials and 59% Gen X).

Other Barna studies suggest declines in other meaningful activities among older Christians. The *Households of Faith* report indicates Boomers are more isolated than younger adults, lack intimate friendships and rarely open their homes to others.[12] Some barriers to engagement could be outside of their control, such as health challenges or absence from social circles one previously occupied during seasons of employment or child-rearing. Others might be a product of generational or personal mindsets that deter an individual from seeing the point of neighborhood groups or their individual involvement. These gaps highlight a need for churches to foster intergenerational community, in an effort to help the Church glean the wisdom of elder Christians and also stir Boomers' hearts toward justice, hospitality, relationship and openness to the insights of others, all of which might stem from or lead to contributions to one's neighborhood.

Let's Talk About: WHY GROUPS WORK

"If you lean in, you get to learn a lot about other people and about yourself. You learn how conditional your love or your grace is or your labels are. It's a very reciprocal experience."
–Greg Russinger, Laundry Love

"What does it take to remove barriers and get folks to do things differently? It takes self-awareness. It takes a different posture."
–Monica Evans, Lupton Center

Group Growth & Retention

Thinking about the most successful group they've been engaged in, the plurality of practicing Christian participants (40%) places the size of that group between 10 and 20 members, in the middle of the range reported to Barna. At either end, about three in 10 say the group was either smaller than 10 members (29%) or exceeded 20 members (31%). Most groups (61%), particularly small ones with more room to grow

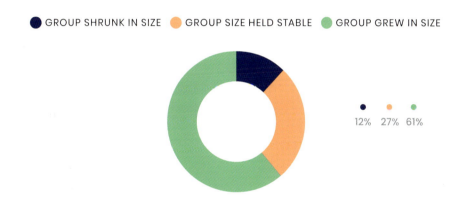

Size of Successful Groups Over Time
Base: practicing Christian community participants

● GROUP SHRUNK IN SIZE   ● GROUP SIZE HELD STABLE   ● GROUP GREW IN SIZE

12%   27%   61%

n=205 U.S. practicing Christian adults who were part of a group, July 25–August 15, 2019. When answering this question, participants were asked to think about the most successful group they'd been a part of.

"The thing that I love about our approach is that people from all different walks are working side-by-side."
—Lynn Heatley, Love Riverside

"We tend to make so many assumptions on how things should be, on how people love and how people communicate, but when you grow in intercultural awareness through repeated encounters that look strange to you, you start to embrace ambiguity more."
—Ben Allin, ESL4Peace

Where Neighborhood Engagement Leads

When people gather to impact communities, participants see benefits within their groups and in their own lives as well. Here's a look at some of the positive results of engagement, many of which coincide.

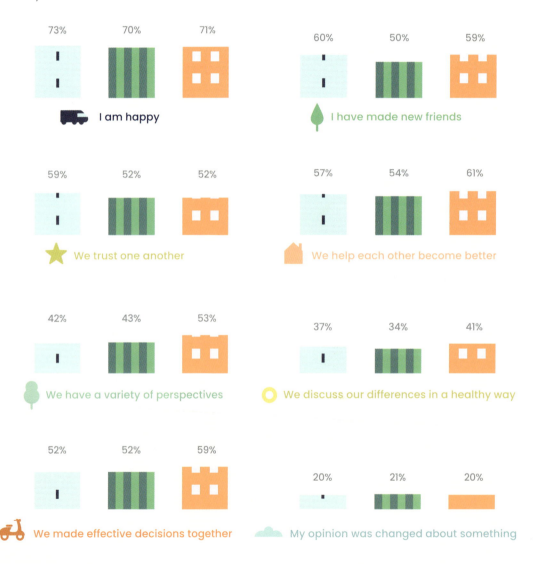

TYPES OF PARTICIPANTS:*
- COMMUNITY
- COMPASSIONATE
- COLLABORATIVE

% who strongly agree

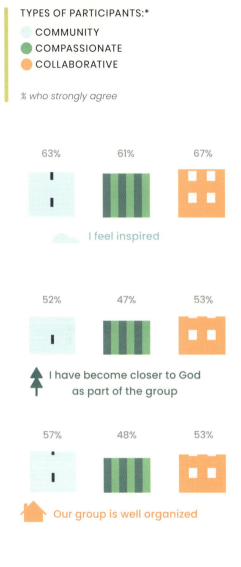

63% / 61% / 67% — I feel inspired

52% / 47% / 53% — I have become closer to God as part of the group

57% / 48% / 53% — Our group is well organized

*See page 14 or see the Methodology for more details about how these groupings were created.

n=205 U.S. practicing Christian adults who were part of a group, July 25–August 19, 2019. Participants were asked to think about the most successful group they'd been a part of.

Overlapping Outcomes

The gains of neighborhood engagement tend to hang together. That is, benefits beget benefits. Happiness is an obvious example, as either a contributor to or a consequence of other positive experiences. People who say their involvement in a successful group added to their personal happiness are more likely than the average to report every other good outcome.

I am happy, and also…
- 74% I made new friends
- 82% I feel inspired
- 71% We trust one another
- 70% We help each other become better
- 61% I have become closer to God

Perhaps of interest to church leaders is the fact that practicing Christians whose group engagement drew them closer to God show signs of increased strength in other relationships, like new friends, healthy communication, diverse perspectives and strong decision-making.

I have become closer to God, and also…
- 84% I feel happy
- 81% I made new friends
- 83% I feel inspired
- 76% We trust one another
- 83% We help each other become better

Where Neighborhood Engagement Leads

(79%), see some increase in size, usually gaining up to 20 additional people (36%), though one-quarter (25%) reports more than 20 people joining their ranks. Another one in four recalls (27%) the group holding steady in size. Few respondents report that successful groups shrunk in membership (12%).

Granted, numerical growth on its own isn't automatically a marker of effectiveness or progress for a group. There are, however, some common factors about groups that experience some level of reported growth, and many are seemingly positive: desires to change or create something, shared values, the financial support of grants, a desire to do good and act on religious beliefs, increased inspiration, more friends and spiritual growth.

When Groups End
Base: practicing Christian community participants

- I'm still a part of this group — 62%
- I moved — 13%
- I could no longer participate because of other responsibilities — 13%
- The group reached its goal and ended — 9%
- The group fell apart — 2%
- I no longer liked the group — 1%
- Other — 5%

n=205 U.S. practicing Christian adults who were part of a group, July 25–August 15, 2019. When answering this question, participants were asked to think about the most successful group they'd been a part of.

Community of ACTION.

THE POWER OF A CHANGED MIND

Participating in a community of action not only benefits the neighborhood as a whole but grows the individual participant as well. In successful groups that lead participants to change their minds about something, three in four practicing Christians say members of the groups also make each other better (76% who changed their mind vs. 47% of others). In many other ways, the data show diversity of thought sharpens members and strengthens groups. And, encouragingly, it seems group members are open to new ideas regardless of their education, income, relationship status, ideology or gender.

Changing one's mind about something occurs more often when members did not know one another before joining (61% who changed their mind vs. 41% of others), perhaps because members took steps outside of their "bubbles"—though friendship (76% vs. 51%) and trust (71% vs. 53%) often follow. So, what draws them toward engagement, if not existing relationships? These practicing Christian participants seem to exhibit greater levels of empathy and interest in justice, being more likely to cite motivations like doing good (70% vs. 53%), helping others (54% vs. 38%), a personal experience of need (34% vs. 19%) or promoting equality (20% vs. 7%). Though members of these successful groups hold many different perspectives (55% vs. 36%), they communicate about disagreements well (52% vs. 30%) and make good decisions (66% vs. 46%). Being together face-to-face perhaps makes this easier to do; 90 percent of those who say their involvement changed their mind indicate the group gathers in person. The size of the group, however, is not a factor; in big or small gatherings, people find something to learn. An evolution of thought is often coupled with spiritual development; 78 percent of those who say their minds were opened to something because of their group participation (vs. 40% of others) also strongly agree they have grown closer to God.

When practicing Christians were asked whether or not they were still a part of this group—the most successful one they've participated in—about six in 10 (62%) report continued involvement. For those who have moved on, the departure is often due to a literal move to a new location (13%) or having too many other responsibilities (13%). One in 10 (9%) says the group simply reached its goal and came to a natural end. As respondents are describing the most successful groups they've known, there are very few accounts of groups falling apart (2%) or participants losing interest (1%).

Rating Overall Group Health

As a more holistic approach to assessing the strength and success of groups engaging and influencing their communities, Barna created a score for healthiness based on combinations of some of the experiences already reported on in this chapter. Specifically, this rating for group health takes into account a participant's level of agreement with the following statements, when considering the most successful group they've been a part of:

- I became closer to God as part of the group
- I made friends as part of the group
- People in the group had a variety of perspectives
- People in the group trusted each other
- There was a bully in the group (*the health score noted disagreement, rather than agreement, with this statement*)
- People in the group talked about their disagreements in a healthy way
- The group members helped each other become better
- The group was well-organized
- The group was able to make effective decisions

Organizational Health of Successful Groups
Base: practicing Christian community participants

● VERY HEALTHY   ● MODERATELY HEALTHY   ● LESS HEALTHY

47%   37%   16%

n=205 U.S. practicing Christian adults who were part of a group, July 25–August 15, 2019. When answering this question, participants were asked to think about the most successful group they'd been a part of.

Those in very healthy groups at least somewhat agreed with more than seven of these items. Overall, nearly half—47 percent—of practicing Christians who have been in successful groups that left some sort of impact on their community provided responses that suggest these were very healthy associations. Though that means a slight majority were involved in moderately or less healthy environments, only 16 percent selected five or fewer of the statements above.

Comparing practicing Christian participants in very healthy groups to practicing Christians in other environments, some general learnings do emerge, many affirming themes already explored in this report.

For instance, doing good is a top motivation for participants (66% practicing Christians in very healthy groups vs. 55% of practicing Christians in moderately and less healthy groups), as well as—expectedly—faith (73% vs. 52%) and personal passions (56% vs. 39%).

Feeling inspired (79% vs. 51% agree) and happy (83% vs. 66% agree) and being stimulated to change one's mind (39% vs. 29% agree) are more common personal experiences for participants in healthy groups.

These strong groups, though they often start small and grow from there, rarely suck participants into becoming busier (62% vs. 52% strongly disagree)—or, perhaps, they are healthy enough environments that respondents do not perceive them as consuming too much of their time.

A Vision That Lasts
A Q&A WITH RUTH EVANS

Q: Let's talk about generational engagement. Have you seen people at certain stages of life or of certain ages engage in community outreach more than others? Who makes up these groups?

A: For sure Millennials and the younger generation; it's just part of their DNA and the way that they view life. I have also seen people who are retired get involved when they feel like they have more time on their hands. Sometimes a stay-at-home spouse might get involved. Honestly though, I have seen very committed and involved people from virtually every stage of life, from college students to young singles to married people with middle school–aged kids.

I think that there are some generational and cultural dynamics that create more awareness for some, like Millennials and Gen Z. But if a certain value is burning in a person's heart, no matter what stage of life they are in, they are going to figure out a way to prioritize getting involved in a group that facilitates that passion.

Q: What have you seen spark or ignite a desire to take action in groups or individuals?

A: I think de-isolation or being close to a person who is impacted by something is one of the biggest motivators. For example, if I am good friends with someone whose dad gets deported, suddenly it's not a philosophy that I'm arguing about anymore.

Ruth Evans is the executive director of Unite, a multi-cultural, multi-denominational movement of churches in the greater Atlanta area. She was also the founder and previous executive director of 2nd Mile, a holistic community development ministry. Evans consults, speaks and trains on topics of reconciliation, culture and community development.

It's a *person* who has been impacted and is hurting as a result of something going wrong in the world.

The closer people venture into others' lives, the more motivated they are to be engaged. You only see brokenness when you get close to it. When you see it from a distance, you have lots of ideas and theories about it, but the closer you get to it and start to feel its impact, the more you realize something has to be done.

Q: **When analyzing successful groups, what are they doing that helps bring about change in the community? What can help groups stay together for a longer period of time?**

A: I think there has to be real people-to-people, relational contact to create change in the world. But often, a group also does have to be combined with some sort of structure or institution that helps it keep moving forward.

There are a lot of people who start groups because they have an emotional response to something, but that emotion soon fizzles out and doesn't last. I think there is a need for really good vision, good support, community connectedness, good clarity, a team who owns the vision together and leadership development and succession. Organizations may be around 20 or 30 years because they have a really good, strong founder, but if they are not very intentional about developing the next tier of leaders, that group will die when the leader dies, especially if it's personality-centric versus vision-centric.

Q: **Should we be empowering people in the Church to start their own volunteer initiatives instead of waiting on their church?**

A: I think churches should be casting the vision and leadership for community involvement and proactively developing leaders within their congregation who could help move the congregation out into those spaces.

While I don't think churches are by any means often the experts in most of these areas, the world around us looks at the Church and either says, "Why aren't you here?" or, "The Church is here in our space, in the places that matter to us."

I believe there should be a sense of

> "The closer people venture into others' lives, the more motivated they are to be engaged."

connectedness and togetherness toward certain initiatives. One church isn't going to connect with every person's passion, but if there are 12 churches in the community that are connected, even if you only have a few people from each church who are interested in a specific cause, now you have a group who can go after something together.

It's hard to describe how incredible it can be in a community where people are led and equipped to live into both the spiritual relationship with Jesus and the social relationship with neighbors. The churches that do that are a powerful force for change in their communities.

What Should the Church's Role Be?

Who do you think is best suited to solve problems in your community?

Respondents look first to the government (about one in three rank this as their number one choice). About one in four says churches and Christian organizations should take the lead, followed by actual members of the community, then charities, businesses and other religious organizations.

Practicing Christians, unsurprisingly, favor the leadership of churches and Christian organizations more (33%), though not much more than the government (31%). Meanwhile, very few non-Christians select the Church as their first option (7%), or even in their top three. They are more likely to identify the government (42%) or citizens (26%) as suitable local problem-solvers.

Among practicing Christians who are participants in groups that impact their

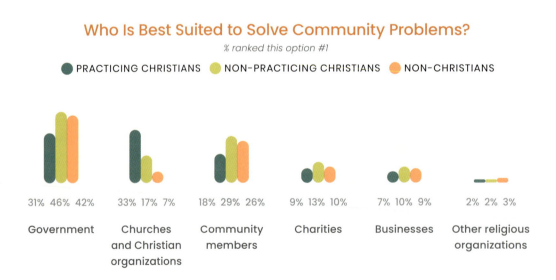

Who Is Best Suited to Solve Community Problems?
% ranked this option #1

● PRACTICING CHRISTIANS ● NON-PRACTICING CHRISTIANS ● NON-CHRISTIANS

Government	Churches and Christian organizations	Community members	Charities	Businesses	Other religious organizations
31% 46% 42%	33% 17% 7%	18% 29% 26%	9% 13% 10%	7% 10% 9%	2% 2% 3%

n=2,500 U.S. adults, July 25–August 15, 2019.

communities, a group we can assume has a level of initiative themselves, more than one-fifth (22% vs. 18% of all practicing Christians) thinks members of the community are best suited to help.

Though the government emerges as the perceived authority on addressing community problems, some openness to the Church's help may be due to the fact that, overall, the majority of U.S. adults are Christians and say people of faith and religious organizations are responsible for the majority of good works in the country. About a quarter of all respondents says good works would still happen without these faith groups. Non-Christians, however, are flipped on this point; just 27 percent attribute charitable works to people of faith, while half (48%) feel these efforts would continue without them. Again, practicing Christians (70%), including those participating in groups that might carry out charitable services (72%), are more inclined to see religious organizations as crucial to good works in the nation.

There are, unsurprisingly, gaps in what, exactly, practicing Christians or non-Christians feel churches and Christian organizations could provide. According to practicing Christians, services for the homeless are seen as the primary offering,

Religion's Relevance in Good Works

● PRACTICING CHRISTIANS   ● NON-PRACTICING CHRISTIANS   ● NON-CHRISTIANS

70% 45% 27%

People of faith and religious organizations provide the majority of good works in the country. If these organizations didn't exist, those good works wouldn't get done.

19% 36% 48%

A majority of good works would still happen even if there were no people of faith or religious organizations to do them.

n=2,500 U.S. adults, July 25–August 15, 2019. Response option "not sure" is not shown above.

though generational programs, either for youth or elderly, are also valued. Many think churches could offer counseling, meet needs for single parents, help fundraise for other charities, support those in addiction recovery or provide other practical services for the community. There is less of a public invitation for the Church to be involved in

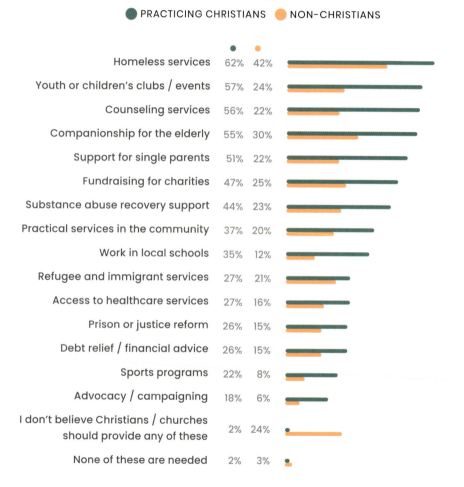

What, If Anything, Does Your Community Need That Churches or Christian Organizations Could Provide?

● PRACTICING CHRISTIANS   ● NON-CHRISTIANS

	Practicing Christians	Non-Christians
Homeless services	62%	42%
Youth or children's clubs / events	57%	24%
Counseling services	56%	22%
Companionship for the elderly	55%	30%
Support for single parents	51%	22%
Fundraising for charities	47%	25%
Substance abuse recovery support	44%	23%
Practical services in the community	37%	20%
Work in local schools	35%	12%
Refugee and immigrant services	27%	21%
Access to healthcare services	27%	16%
Prison or justice reform	26%	15%
Debt relief / financial advice	26%	15%
Sports programs	22%	8%
Advocacy / campaigning	18%	6%
I don't believe Christians / churches should provide any of these	2%	24%
None of these are needed	2%	3%

n=1,505 U.S. practicing Christian adults and 264 non-Christian U.S. adults who were part of a group, July 25–August 15, 2019.

schools, healthcare, prison reform, refugee care, financial services, sports programs or local advocacy. Consistently, non-Christians are less likely than Christians to seek the Church's provision for community needs. One in four non-Christians (24%) doesn't

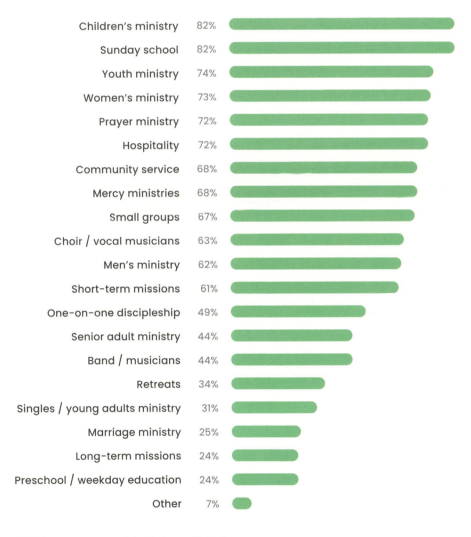

Programs Churches Offer

Program	%
Children's ministry	82%
Sunday school	82%
Youth ministry	74%
Women's ministry	73%
Prayer ministry	72%
Hospitality	72%
Community service	68%
Mercy ministries	68%
Small groups	67%
Choir / vocal musicians	63%
Men's ministry	62%
Short-term missions	61%
One-on-one discipleship	49%
Senior adult ministry	44%
Band / musicians	44%
Retreats	34%
Singles / young adults ministry	31%
Marriage ministry	25%
Long-term missions	24%
Preschool / weekday education	24%
Other	7%

n=508 U.S. Protestant pastors, July 25–August 13, 2019.

think churches are needed in any of these areas.

Pastors' responses give us a picture of what churches actually offer and their practical ability to meet some of these community needs. Their primary focus is, expectedly, on key services and programs within the congregation: children's ministry, Sunday school, youth and women's ministries and so on. Offering prayer and hospitality is also a common offering. From there, the focus begins to shift outward, including community services and "mercy ministries," something nearly seven in 10 pastors say is provided, and which might account for some of the problems adults hope churches might address. Singles and marriage ministries, long-term missions and pre-school are more specialty offerings, selected by a minority of pastors, about one in four.

Cultural Trends Shaping Our Neighborhoods

A Q&A WITH GABE LYONS

Q: We're living in a time when people mistrust institutions and the Church has a mixed reputation. How could Christians engaging their neighborhoods address some of that?

A: There's a great opportunity for individuals who belong to churches to be more tangibly present in their communities. Because people do distrust institutions, the best opportunity to change those perceptions is through one-on-one interactions.

We've perhaps gotten comfortable in our institutions and just believed that the Church would always be respected in American culture. Now, we realize that's not holding, especially in the younger generations. Not only does the Church lack respect, but in many ways, it is receiving antagonism from those who disagree with Christian beliefs and don't see the Church as helpful in society.

As Christians move out into the community, through tangible interactions with

Gabe Lyons is the coauthor of *Good Faith* and *unChristian*, with Barna president David Kinnaman, and author of *The Next Christians*. He is the founder of Q, a learning community that helps Christian leaders engage our cultural moment. The Q Conference annually convenes thousands of leaders from all industries and the global Q Commons event unites 140 cities and over 10,000 people each fall. Lyons speaks to over 100,000 people each year on topics such as equipping the next generation, cultural issues and research related to the intersection of faith and public life. He lives in Nashville with his wife, Rebekah, and their four children.

their neighbors, with their colleagues at work, their shop owners and people engaged in all walks of life, they're able to bring a taste of God's love and the Church's mission into those spaces.

> *"Because people do distrust institutions, the best opportunity to change those perceptions is through one-on-one interactions."*

Q: This research and report is launching in 2020, an election year. How are some political shifts, such as rising interest in socialism, affecting the way that people, especially Christians, engage with their community? How does the national discourse influence the way we meet needs on a local level?

A: This is a double-edged sword, as this conversation on socialism has an opportunity embedded in it. The opportunity is that, at a higher level than ever before, people are recognizing the needs of the community, such as addressing mental health, helping the homeless or helping people recover from addictions and find long-term healing. They're realizing how much our children need support in their studies, tutoring and opportunities after school. So, many are turning to the government to provide solutions in the absence of the Church's presence. This invites the Church to take note and to show up in their communities in even more tangible ways.

One of the Church's great opportunities is to partner more with existing social sector organizations who are meeting needs in the community so that the Church can be a presence in the midst of what's already taking place.

When we do that, people start to realize and recognize what has always been true: that faith and religion tend to motivate philanthropy and volunteerism at a higher level than lack of faith or religion.

Q: How would you advise Christians to find the balance between seeing themselves as empowered to be the Church, but also committing themselves to be involved with the Church, instead of just doing good works independently? How can pastors encourage congregants to take the initiative to do something outside ministry programs, while also drawing them deeper into the faith community?

A: I think that pastors must teach, train, equip and disciple their people to understand that being the Church is not about attending the Sunday morning experience or showing up in the church building. It's largely about what's happening every day of the week, wherever they've already been called. There's theological training or theological education that has to happen at a higher degree within the Church to empower this kind of thinking so that churches aren't competing with outside volunteer activities, but instead embracing and celebrating all of the ways their people are involved in the community.

I think the more this is modeled from church programming platforms—celebrating volunteerism, elevating people who are leading different activities in the community or solving problems and doing good—it starts to build within the church culture a sense that "This is where we come to be sent out"—not "This is where we come just to be filled up."

A good follow-up to the first area of teaching is asking, *How do we actually create true community?* We have this misconception that community is found by creating a small group that sits in a circle and has conversation. Actually, community is only formed at the deepest levels when we work and do things together. The people you find yourself actually in community with are the ones with whom you're sharing common goals, doing things together or sacrificing for one another. Therefore, this very act of serving in the community becomes what builds internal strength within the Church. Serving doesn't actually take you away from the Church; it draws you into closer relationship with the people you're serving alongside.

Inspiring Action:

HOW CHURCHES NURTURE—AND RELEASE— PEOPLE WHO WANT TO DO GOOD

Though pastors' top ministry priorities—worship (29%) and teaching (27%)—center around Sunday services, lay-led initiatives mesh well with many of their stated aims. It's not hard to see how congregants' involvement in groups that act in and impact their neighborhoods could provide opportunities for effective outreach and evangelism, relationship building and, of course, community engagement, all ranked among pastors' priorities. And while these groups might gather outside of formal church structures and teaching, such independent initiatives could also be encouraged as part of discipleship—the number-one priority for one in four pastors (25%). These community groups not only may lead to hands-on, in-person experiences in redemptive work but also, as practicing Christians tell us, contribute to personal spiritual growth (*see page 85*), as well as myriad other benefits.

The research findings may be preaching to the pulpit here; pastors already see tremendous value in lay-led initiatives—in fact, the majority prefers them to new church programs (40% agree strongly, 52% agree somewhat) and feels that lay people taking on responsibility is a mark of an increasingly healthy church (68% agree strongly, 28% agree somewhat). Accordingly, nearly all (97%) can think of at least one congregant-led community that has had a positive impact on their

> The majority of pastors feels that lay people taking on responsibility is a mark of an increasingly healthy church

church, with more than two-thirds (68%) saying *all* of them have been a benefit.

Though pastors still assume a lot of personal responsibility in various aspects of sharing the gospel or doing good works, their responses indicate they are counting on everybody in their congregation to take up the mantle of representing the Church in the community. In some cases, they're more likely to place responsibility on the whole church as a body than on their church staff or even on themselves. Among the things they especially hope any member might embrace are evangelism and outreach (85%), showing others how to live as Christians (79%), helping the poor (77%), teaching others about God (60%) and giving practical help to those in sickness, transition or crisis (59%). Overall, this emphasizes the theme that church leaders endorse empowering laity.

But the reality is that pastors may be hoping for much from laity without offering much in the way of growth opportunities. For example,

Top Church Priorities

● RANKED #1   ● RANKED #2   ● RANKED #3

Priority	#1	#2	#3
Worship	29%	11%	10%
Teaching / preaching	27%	17%	13%
Discipleship	25%	28%	13%
Evangelism or outreach	11%	19%	22%
Community engagement	5%	11%	18%
Relationship building	2%	7%	8%
Missions	1%	6%	15%
Civic engagement / activism	0%	1%	1%

n=508 U.S. Protestant pastors, July 25–August 13, 2019.

"I Prefer Lay Initiatives to New Church Programs"

- AGREE STRONGLY: 40%
- AGREE SOMEWHAT: 52%
- DISAGREE SOMEWHAT: 8%
- DISAGREE STRONGLY: 0%

"For Our Church to Be Healthier, Lay People Must Take More Responsibility"

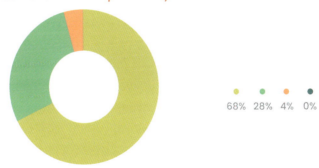

- AGREE STRONGLY: 68%
- AGREE SOMEWHAT: 28%
- DISAGREE SOMEWHAT: 4%
- DISAGREE STRONGLY: 0%

"My Church Leadership Is Good at Developing New Leaders"

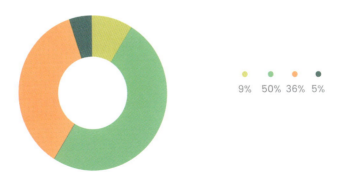

- AGREE STRONGLY: 9%
- AGREE SOMEWHAT: 50%
- DISAGREE SOMEWHAT: 36%
- DISAGREE STRONGLY: 5%

n=508 U.S. Protestant pastors, July 25–August 13, 2019.

just 9 percent strongly agree their team is good at developing new leaders; another half (50%) somewhat agree. Whether because of high standards or low investment, 41 percent of pastors feel their churches are doing a poor job when it comes to leadership development.

In this chapter, we'll gauge how pastors perceive and interact with groups going out into the community and learn about some of the factors that can continue to strengthen those relationships, contribute to church service and set lay leaders up for success.

Responding to Parishioner Passions

One in five pastors (19%) believes that lay-led volunteer efforts hinge on the group's passion for the cause, a factor that ties only with good communication (20%) as a perceived key to success. This aligns with data from the survey of practicing Christians, which repeatedly underscores shared passion as a foundation for successful groups. So, what do pastors presently do when members of their congregations come forward about their passions and ideas to help others, something most pastors say happens at least occasionally (55% sometimes, 25% often)?

For the most part, pastors are open to these suggestions, greeting them with curiosity and encouragement. Often, pastors respond to such ideas with two questions:

1. What will you [the congregant] personally do to get this started?
2. What do you need from us to make this happen?

This is true regardless of the pastor's background or demographic or the size of the church where they work. And this may speak to one of the main reasons we see such high expressed support of lay-led initiatives: Busy spiritual leaders aren't exactly looking to be the point

ENVIRONMENTS WHERE PARTICIPANTS EXPERIENCE SPIRITUAL GROWTH

More than half of practicing Christian participants say their involvement in a successful group in their neighborhood helped them grow closer to God. Church leaders wondering how community groups connect to their discipleship efforts should be encouraged by this news, as well as the many other positive group and personal experiences correlated with spiritual growth. Compared to those who did not at least somewhat agree that their engagement drew them closer to God, these faithful members are more likely to:

- meet with their group in person (86% vs. 66%)
- be in a group that grew in size (67% vs. 42%)
- be involved because of religious beliefs (75% vs. 23%), passions (52% vs. 27%), a longing to help people help themselves (48% vs. 27%) or biblical instruction (40% vs. 4%)
- feel happy (95% vs. 85%) and inspired (91% vs. 67%)
- be in a group with a variety of perspectives (89% vs. 68%) and, relatedly, say they changed their mind about something (43% vs. 9%)
- be in a group where people trusted one another (96% vs. 72%), talked healthily about disagreements (75% vs. 57%), made each other better (95% vs. 66%) and made friends (92% vs. 69%)
- be in a well-organized group (92% vs. 72%) that made effective decisions (94% vs. 77%)
- still be a part of this successful group (68% vs. 43%)

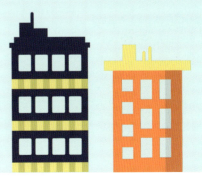

person for another program. They may see obvious gains for the community in encouraging the altruistic agency of church members, as well as acknowledging that this alleviates pressure on ministry time and resources to meet perceived needs of the neighborhood.

Even so, they aren't entirely convinced that their support *matters* to said groups. Thinking of community groups that have existed as an extension of their congregations—most of which (85%) started outside of a church or other institution—nearly half of pastors (46%) say these

Some of Pastors' Responses When People Have Suggestions for Helping Others

- Offer positive feedback & encouragement — 28%
- Ask how they will get it started — 26%
- Support, advise or promote — 24%
- Express openness to the idea — 23%
- Offer to help or take it on together — 16%
- Evaluate the idea & level of involvement — 16%
- Connect them to existing ministries or others who are interested — 9%
- Join them in prayer — 8%
- Encourage them to get others or a team involved — 7%
- Allow God to use them in their calling — 6%
- Present the idea to others (the board, missions department, congregation) — 6%
- Other — 4%

n=503 U.S. Protestant pastors, July 25–August 13, 2019. These options are coded from pastors' open-ended responses.

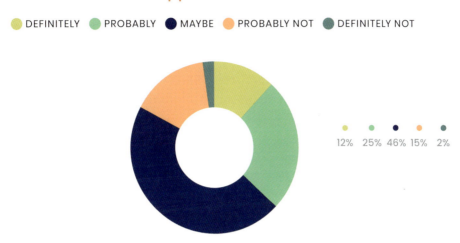

n=453 U.S. Protestant pastors who have people from their church involved in groups outside of the church's programs, July 25–August 13, 2019.

groups would only "maybe" have been more successful if they had had more church support. Some think additional support would have had a decided impact (25% probably, 12% definitely), while 17 percent don't feel it would have made a difference (2% definitely not, 15% probably not).

Among pastors who agree that lay-led efforts could have benefited from greater church backing, there is a sense that the strongest show of support is to spread the word, by giving a voice to or advertising the group (37%) or getting more people involved (35%). One-third (32%) says financial assistance is a way their church could have offered more tangible help. Interestingly, some of the most accessible forms of ministerial or spiritual support—such as prayer (5%), encouragement (3%) or simply providing connections to related groups (2%)—aren't mentioned as often. This study can't say whether that's because pastors don't see these as priorities or responsibilities, or that they don't see these options as ones that would have particularly affected the success of community groups.

One of the traits that consistently surfaces among pastors who are supportive of lay-led efforts is that they are newer to ministry in general or to their church specifically. Pastors who have had shorter ministry or church tenures (and thus typically younger pastors) are more likely to prefer lay-led groups to new church programs and to see these communities as a mark of church health.

How Can Churches Lend Support to Groups?
% who feel support would help groups be more successful

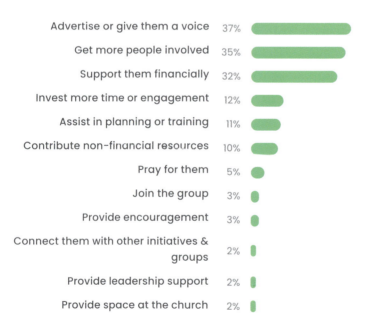

Response	%
Advertise or give them a voice	37%
Get more people involved	35%
Support them financially	32%
Invest more time or engagement	12%
Assist in planning or training	11%
Contribute non-financial resources	10%
Pray for them	5%
Join the group	3%
Provide encouragement	3%
Connect them with other initiatives & groups	2%
Provide leadership support	2%
Provide space at the church	2%

n=164 U.S. Protestant pastors who have people from their church involved in groups outside of the church's programs and feel church support would help groups succeed, July 25–August 13, 2019. These options are coded from pastors' open-ended responses.

Meanwhile, though more seasoned pastors may not see themselves as champions of these community groups, they are, by their own assessment, doing a good job developing new leaders. They are also more likely than less experienced pastors to report positive experiences with independent groups and to say that members of their churches are modeling Christlike lives and frequently have ideas for how to help others. The gap in favor toward lay-led volunteering may have more to do with vocabulary or generational context, rather than pastors' actual interactions with or backing of what the researchers are referring to as communities of action. Further, these data differences could be regarded as possible collaboration points or areas of growth, where greener pastors' passion might be linked with more veteran pastors' expertise in empowering and raising up churchgoers.

Becoming Attuned to Community Needs

More than half the time (54%), pastors say that lay-led volunteering groups are borne of a desire to address an unmet need in the community. It follows, then, that church leaders who believe they are very well aware of community needs are more likely to report lay-led initiatives among their congregations (91% vs. 76%).

Relatedly, pastors of churches where congregants are involved in groups that impact their neighbors also tend to report offering more formal church programming for mercy ministries or community service. Thus, it doesn't appear that these community groups are started simply because related ministries do not already exist in a church. It is likely *because* churches offer these ministries or foster these needs that people are more focused on helping those outside of their churches. This syncs well with other findings from this study that suggest passion for a particular cause or community compounds rather than competes across contexts. An awareness of needs begets an awareness of needs; a willingness to serve begets a willingness to serve. Indeed,

> Church leaders who believe they are very well aware of community needs are more likely to report lay-led initiatives among their congregations

Pastors' Top Explanations for Why Groups Begin

To address a need	54%
Passion or vision for a cause	17%
Love for Jesus / response to faith / moved by the Spirit	16%
Desire to help others / have a heart to serve	14%
Like-minded people coming together over a common interest	7%
The church is not able to fill that need outside of current ministry structure	5%
Passion to lead / rally others	5%
Fellowship	3%
Desire to make a difference	3%
Involves leadership of church	2%
Other	5%

n=448 U.S. Protestant pastors who have people from their church involved in groups outside of the church's programs, July 25–August 13, 2019.

Let's Talk About: PARTNERING WITH THE COMMUNITY

"I think it's critically important for churches to lead some of the initiative and vision. There are dreamers and there are doers, and there's a Venn diagram where they cross."
—Emily Gibson, Thrivent Action Teams

"I want to encourage church leaders to begin to measure the outcomes and look at what it would mean to reorient how we evaluate church leadership and pastors, not just by how well they lead the members who are already part of our church, but how well they help us to serve our communities."
—Glenn Barth, Good Cities

pastors who know community needs well are much less likely to sense that there is an inevitable tradeoff between community service and church service (51% vs. 76% who don't know community needs well).

These pastors might be well-acquainted with local needs merely because they make an effort to track them; 62 percent in this category,

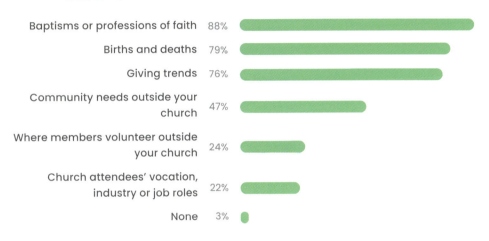

Information Churches Track or Collect Each Year

- Baptisms or professions of faith — 88%
- Births and deaths — 79%
- Giving trends — 76%
- Community needs outside your church — 47%
- Where members volunteer outside your church — 24%
- Church attendees' vocation, industry or job roles — 22%
- None — 3%

n=508 U.S. Protestant pastors, July 25–August 13, 2019.

"What do you have going on in your own backyard that the Lord might want you to become involved in or partner with?"
–Lynn Heatley, Love Riverside

"I think there are two good reasons to partner with the Church. Number one is financial, because fundraising as a small group is really hard. Number two is that it helps get the word out."
–Joy Harty, Sixty Feet

compared to 47 percent of pastors overall, report collecting this type of information at least once every year. These ministries also keep a close eye on members' volunteering or vocational tendencies, knowledge that might help connect congregants' and lay leaders' passions and skillsets with particular groups or causes, whether inside or outside the church.

It's worth noting that churches where pastors feel so integrated with their communities might just be better able to afford this kind of reach and awareness—meaning, they are more likely to be leaders in larger churches (250+ members) with bigger operating budgets ($500,000 or more annually), two factors that consistently correlate with a pastor's capacity to generate communities of action and support the neighborhoods they reach.

Confronting the Fear of Losing Volunteers

Church leaders still harbor some hesitations about seeing members take initiative to serve their community beyond church programs. Overall, nearly all pastors (94%) say that, without exception, their congregation should be helping those in need—though, many might add, they hope it doesn't distract volunteers from church purposes.

Let's Talk About: PARTNERING WITH THE COMMUNITY

"Churches need to be strong enough to be willing to let people pursue a calling. Kingdom building is not a competition. Encourage people to join something that is being done in the community."
—Qualitative study participant

A main concern is that if attendees spend more time volunteering to meet needs in the community, they will have less time to give toward ministry initiatives. Three out of five pastors (60%) tell Barna they see a tradeoff between individuals' engagement in service in the community and service in church, and nearly half (46%) say the same for community service and small group participation. Interestingly, pastors in larger churches (250 or more attendees), where you might assume a greater amount of resources and volunteers, are even more likely to insist that community service detracts from church involvement.

It's natural and even wise for pastors to prize any eager members and helping hands they can find. After all, 85 percent say their church is at least sometimes short of volunteers for its programs. But though a large majority of leaders (94%) says people in their congregation are too busy, responses from some of the most involved practicing Christians indicate that busyness isn't always the obstacle pastors assume it is.

> Responses from some of the most involved practicing Christians indicate that busyness isn't always the obstacle pastors assume it is

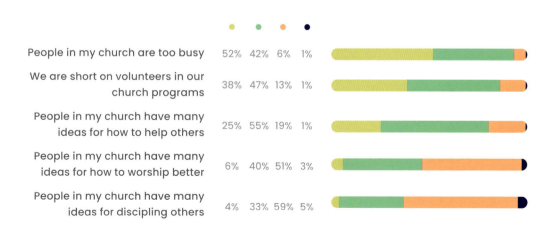

Capacity & Initiative of Congregations

● OFTEN ● SOMETIMES ● SELDOM ● NEVER

	Often	Sometimes	Seldom	Never
People in my church are too busy	52%	42%	6%	1%
We are short on volunteers in our church programs	38%	47%	13%	1%
People in my church have many ideas for how to help others	25%	55%	19%	1%
People in my church have many ideas for how to worship better	6%	40%	51%	3%
People in my church have many ideas for discipling others	4%	33%	59%	5%

n=508 U.S. Protestant pastors, July 25–August 13, 2019.

When thinking of the most successful group they've participated in, regardless of their role, most practicing Christians don't report that their church involvement actually decreased because of their engagement with an outside group (94% say "no"). Granted, this is the subjective report of congregants, and wouldn't have great impact if respondents weren't very involved with a church to begin with—but

Pastors Feel Community Service Requires Time Tradeoffs

"Have you seen a tradeoff between these activities? That is, a person does less of one to do more of the other?"

● YES, THERE IS A TRADEOFF   ● NO, PEOPLE DO BOTH EQUALLY

	Yes	No
Community service & serving church ministries	60%	40%
Community service & small group participation	46%	54%
Small group participation & serving church ministries	40%	60%

n=508 U.S. Protestant pastors, July 25–August 13, 2019.

Let's Talk About: NURTURING CHRISTIANS' PASSIONS

"What is the unique contribution of the local church? If this type of community of action is part of the wiring of the foundation and the culture, then hopefully the individuals and families realize that they must bear responsibility and witness to that, wherever they may be."

–Greg Russinger, *Laundry Love*

"The role of the pastor is to equip God's people for witness and service. When this is done well, the gifts and callings of the church come alive through service, blessing many in the community. An engaged people of faith reflect the servanthood of Jesus. Friendships are formed and the incarnational witness of God's people grows."

–Glenn Barth, *Good Cities*

it is significant considering that a majority (57%), particularly group leaders (67% of those who hosted, taught, advised or coached a group) and founders (91% of those who started a group), volunteers in a church every week. In fact, they're more likely to say they have decreased involvement in other realms of life such as school, work, family or friends, though even this tradeoff is rare. Overall, 57 percent of

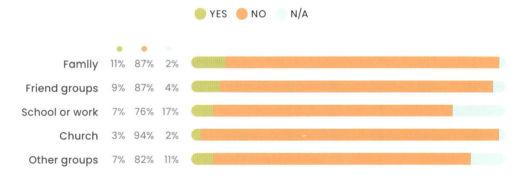

… But That Isn't the Experience of Group Participants

"Because of your involvement in any of these groups, did your involvement in any of the following decrease?"

Base: practicing Christian community participants

● YES ● NO ● N/A

	YES	NO	N/A
Family	11%	87%	2%
Friend groups	9%	87%	4%
School or work	7%	76%	17%
Church	3%	94%	2%
Other groups	7%	82%	11%

n=205 U.S. practicing Christian adults who were a part of a group, July 25–August 15, 2019. When answering this question, participants were asked to think about the most successful group they'd been a part of.

"Many amazing people of faith are serving God in their Monday-to-Friday jobs. My heart is that they would feel supported, prayed for and encouraged by their local congregation's leadership team. That strengthens the community in a whole different way."

–Lynn Heatley, Love Riverside

"It has to start with the leadership casting a vision for their city and their community. Once the congregation gets a hold of what God wants to do outside of their church walls, they're going to say, 'I think that's it.'"

–Stephanie Wieber, Palau Association

practicing Christian participants say that it's "not true at all" that being in a group made them too busy, a proportion that climbs to two-thirds among those engaging only at a participant level (64%). Even for leaders, half (49%) say their level of busyness was not impacted by being in the group.

Many participants of groups also feel that they are still finding ways to use their talents and skills *through* their church as well. Half (51%) strongly agree this is the case, and another 39 percent say it's somewhat true. Seven in 10 (29% strongly + 42% somewhat agree), and especially younger practicing Christians (39% Millennials and 42% Gen X strongly agree), would like to deepen their vocational connection to their church. Here, too, some of the busiest group participants are some of the most likely to say they're applying their skillsets in a church context. It's possible this could be another thing contributing to that sense of busyness, but even so, it's not apparent that these individuals are backing out of either their church or community engagement. And it may be that this vocational encouragement through their church also spurs them on in applying their skills and passions outwardly to benefit their neighbors.

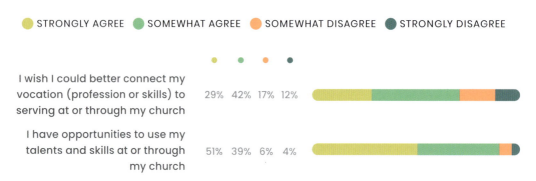

Vocation & the Church
Base: practicing Christian community participants

● STRONGLY AGREE ● SOMEWHAT AGREE ● SOMEWHAT DISAGREE ● STRONGLY DISAGREE

	Strongly Agree	Somewhat Agree	Somewhat Disagree	Strongly Disagree
I wish I could better connect my vocation (profession or skills) to serving at or through my church	29%	42%	17%	12%
I have opportunities to use my talents and skills at or through my church	51%	39%	6%	4%

n=392 U.S. practicing Christian adults who were a part of a group, July 25–August 15, 2019.

Barriers to involvement, inside or outside the Church, may have less to do with busyness and more to do with initiative or culture fit. Among practicing Christians who've never been a part of a group with community impact, there are still many causes that inspire passion or concern, and a majority says they would at least consider joining a group to address them (42% definitely + 30% probably + 21% maybe). So what's holding them back? Mainly, they can't find a group they like (30%). About one in five (17%) does acknowledge they don't have time for this kind of activity, but a similar proportion says they just haven't gotten around to joining a group (18%) or would rather give money than get involved (12%).

Where there is interest, churches may have an opportunity to connect people with existing groups that are meeting neighborhood needs. When asked if they'd like a church's help in finding or joining a group that addresses the causes that concern them, practicing Christian non-participants are quite open to the idea (35% definitely + 25% probably + 31% maybe).

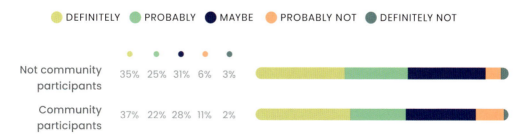

n=1,005 U.S. practicing Christian adults, July 25–August 15, 2019.

Navigating the Intersection of Church Leadership & Community Engagement

A Q&A WITH BECCA STEVENS

Q: When it began, did Thistle Farms resemble the lay-led initiatives we are researching here? Today, who is served, who is serving and how are they coming alongside one another?

A: I would not use the language of lay-led as that is a pretty "churchy" word, and Thistle Farms is not a religious organization but a not-for-profit. I would consider it survivor-informed, with a communal vision influenced by the community of people working together. I never wanted Thistle Farms to be something we "do for women," but instead, something we "do with women." Women survivors currently are in leadership positions in more than half of the departments run by Thistle Farms.

Q: In your experience as a priest, what have you seen as the primary motivation or inspiration that drives the formation of

Becca Stevens

A priest, author, speaker and social entrepreneur, Stevens is the president of Thistle Farms, a multifaceted international nonprofit. She founded the organization more than 20 years ago to provide a sanctuary and healing for women survivors of prostitution, trafficking and addiction not historically served. Stevens leads important conversations across the country by speaking, writing, and heading a national network of like-minded organizations. She has founded seven justice organizations and helped raise more than $50 million. The *New York Times*, PBS, ABC World News, NPR, CNN and the White House have all highlighted Stevens and her work.

congregant-led groups that impact the neighborhood?

A: It is the power and agility of small community. That is where relationships are built, and that is where we find deep meaning, accountability and purpose.

Q: How can church leaders tap into the vocational skills and passions of their congregants and enable them to use those passions to take action, even independent of the church, for the common good?

A: I would say avoid the trap of sending everything to committees managed by the church, where inspiration gets bogged down. Instead, help small groups form with the freedom to act. The idea that the whole church has to be on board before anything gets done makes institutions less effective.

> "Lead with mission and let it form your worship, your stewardship and your evangelism."

Q: Data show that church leaders are afraid of competing for their congregants' time, but time actually isn't a significant factor in an individual's decision to engage in an activity—church-led or not. It's more often passion for a cause that drives people to action. What would you say to church leaders who are concerned about losing their volunteers to outside initiatives?

A: *Be* a mission, *with* a church. Don't fall into the trap of feeling like you are a church trying to support various missions. Lead with mission and let it form your worship, your stewardship and your evangelism.

Q: How have you supported congregants in what they do outside the church and what advice would you give to other churches or why is it meaningful or helpful for them to support their congregants' passions?

A: I don't know that I do a good job of supporting congregants, but I do these three things intentionally:

1. I am conscious of who the "we" is when I preach. If I am not preaching from the perspective of being in need of mercy and justice, I am not doing the work;
2. I hold up great examples of mission by individuals in the community to inspire action, not judgement;
3. I keep things simple and transparent so more time and energy can go toward the mission.

Q: How do you seek to support lay people in the volunteer work they're already doing or share info about the platform they already have?

A: Mostly through announcements, social media, weekly newsletters, Eventbrite and an email list. We share, we post, we talk! 🟢

Conclusion

PARTNERING WITH CHURCHGOERS FOR NEIGHBORHOOD IMPACT

If you are a pastor, volunteer coordinator or other church leader who picked up *Better Together*, you may be wondering: *What do I do with this data?* Perhaps you're inclined to interpret the research about these generous, independent groups as an admonishment (or even an excuse) for churches to *do less*.

That might be the case, if you're thinking strictly of organizing church-led programs—and perhaps, for your ministry, doing less in this regard would be a wise or welcome shift! But, in another sense, this study should prompt all churches to *do more* in terms of intimately knowing the needs and neighbors in their community. It suggests they *do more* to listen to the concerns, fuel the passions and support the gifts of churchgoers. It urges they *do more* to equip laity to understand and live out the gospel beyond church walls and contexts.

You may have heard people say, "Work smarter, not harder," a well-known professional mantra and productivity hack; this idea might apply well to this conversation. Decentralizing Christians' efforts to meet community needs is strategic, compassionate and Kingdom-minded "smart work," involving a commitment from clergy, lay leaders and everyday churchgoers to be good stewards of their resources, time and talents. As Ephesians 4: 16 states, "As each part does its own special work, it helps the other parts grow, so that the whole body is healthy and growing and full of love." (NLT)

Here is some of the work and growth that may lie ahead for you and your church:

Get to know your neighborhood with your congregation.

According to pastors' responses, there appears to be a natural overlap between the churches where leaders understand community needs and churches where congregants have agency to impact their communities. Has your team put down neighborhood roots and developed strong partnerships with local officials, schools, organizations and other churches? How do you listen to, monitor and educate yourselves and your congregation about the pressing issues in your area?

People who are already sitting in your Sunday services could be guides in understanding local problems and might already be interested or invested in the solutions. Further, some Christians who aren't yet participating in volunteer groups would be open to doing so if their churches pointed them in the right direction. Get serious about recording and sharing such information across your church, perhaps even helping congregants map their gifts and concerns to connect with other individuals who share them and groups that address them. Perhaps you might note their goals and motivations, hoping to place or move them along the spectrum of participation: from community, to compassionate, to collaborative participants. Continue to collect data and stories about active groups to learn from their experiments and successes. This will not only strengthen your church's own formal outreach and mission opportunities, but also encourage and demonstrate the reach of your congregation.

Carefully consider when your church should step up or step aside.

How should pastors, elders and staff members determine when to pursue church-led initiatives or support lay-led groups? There will be cases in which one, both or neither make the most sense. You might also consider a range of possible ministry responses when opting to support laity, including financial donations, shared meeting spaces, themed sermons, announcements and advertisements, forums, volunteer coordination, a season of prayer and so on. Engaging with the community should involve a process of discernment, undertaken with stakeholders and experts who have knowledge of the needs, church strengths and callings, financial resources and the possible reception or result in the neighborhood. Establish a process by which church leadership can agree upon which next step(s) to prioritize. Aim to never duplicate efforts; rather, initiate new ones or celebrate existing ones.

> Aim to never duplicate efforts; rather, initiate new ones or celebrate existing ones

Recognize the many other needs being met through lay-led community groups.

In a practical sense, volunteer gatherings might address poverty, protect vulnerable youth, clean community spaces, raise funds for non-profits, advocate for equality or support local arts. These associations can also have other benefits which are less tangible: stronger faith, new perspectives, deeper friendships.

Barna studies underscore how young adults in the U.S. long for meaningful relationships, vocational purpose and mentorship. They are eager to see the Church in action, taking its justice responsibilities seriously. Additionally, older generations struggle to build community, particularly with those who see the world differently, and may not grasp how they can be a valuable, active part of the Church's local presence. By nurturing congregant passions and volunteer groups, ministries also nurture believers to be formed and fortified in other important ways—perhaps more organically than is possible in church services and environments alone.

See passionate Christians as a renewable, not finite, resource.

Rallying Christians to serve their communities, with or without a formal church program, may raise a common clergy fear: that you might wear out, distract or lose your best ministry volunteers. Understandable. For the most part, however, this study suggests committed volunteers don't feel taxed for time or pressured to choose between their church or community service. Further, your congregants have a unique, personal chance to connect with non-Christian neighbors who often put more faith in individual community members than in the local church. Volunteer group participants can act as a valuable extension of your place of worship and build the credibility of the Church at large through relationships and good works.

Ultimately, you can't control how your current or potential volunteers use their time—but you can focus on making, teaching and empowering disciples who show up wholly and generously, in church and all the other dimensions of their lives.

APPENDIX

Notes

1. Barna Group. "Church Dropouts Have Risen to 94%—But What About Those Who Stay?" September 4, 2019. https://www.barna.com/research/resilient-disciples/.

2. Barna Group. "Almost Half of Practicing Christian Millennials Say Evangelism Is Wrong." February 5, 2019. https://www.barna.com/research/millennials-oppose-evangelism/

3. Barna Group. "Atheism Doubles Among Generation Z." January 24, 2018. https://www.barna.com/research/atheism-doubles-among-generation-z/

4. Quoted in *Pittsburgh Post-Gazette*. "Obituary: Fred Rogers." March 2, 2003. Accessed at https://www.legacy.com/obituaries/PostGazette/obituary.aspx?n=Fred-Rogers&pid=833599.

5. Jonathan Merritt. "Saint Fred." *The Atlantic*. November 22, 2015. https://www.theatlantic.com/politics/archive/2015/11/mister-rogers-saint/416838/; David Dark. "In the age of Trump, can Mr. Rogers help us manage our anger?" *America*. April 19, 2017. https://www.americamagazine.org/politics-society/2017/04/19/age-trump-can-mr-rogers-help-us-manage-our-anger.

6. Tom Junod. "My Friend Mister Rogers." *The Atlantic*. December 2019. https://www.theatlantic.com/magazine/archive/2019/12/what-would-mister-rogers-do/600772/

7. Barna Group. "U.S. Adults Have Few Friends—and They're Mostly Alike." October 23, 2018. https://www.barna.com/research/friends-loneliness/.

8. Barna Group. "Americans Struggle to Talk Across Divides." March 9, 2016. https://www.barna.com/research/americans-struggle-to-talk-across-divides/.

9. Luther, Martin. *Luther's Little Instruction Book (the Small Catechism of Martin Luther)*. Champaign, Ill.: Boulder, Colo.: Project Gutenberg; NetLibrary, 1994.

10. D.R. Krathwohl, B.S. Bloom and B.B. Masia. *Taxonomy of Educational Objectives: Handbook II: Affective Domain*. New York: David McKay Co, 1964.

11. Pierrecarlo Valdesolo and David DeSteno. "Synchrony and the Social Tuning of Compassion." *Emotion* Vol. 11 No. 2 (2011): 262–266. https://static1.squarespace.com/static/52853b8ae4b0a6c35d3f8e9d/t/528d25dae4b059766439b87e/1384981978770/synchrony-and-the-social-tuning-of-compassion.pdf.

12. Barna Group. *Households of Faith*. Ventura, CA: Barna Group, 2019.

APPENDIX

Methodology

This quantitative study consisted of two online surveys.

The first was a survey of 2,500 U.S. adults conducted from July 25–August 19, 2019. The sample breakdown was as follows: 1,505 U.S. practicing Christians (meaning they self-identify as Christian, say their faith is very important in their life and have attended church within the past month other than for a holiday service or for a special event, such as a wedding or funeral), and 995 adults who are not practicing Christians. The margin of error for this sample is +/- 1.7 percent at the 95 percent confidence level.

Researchers set quotas to obtain a minimum readable sample by a variety of demographic factors and weighted the two samples by region, ethnicity, education, age and gender to reflect their natural presence in the American population (using U.S. Census Bureau data for comparison). Partly by nature of using an online panel, these respondents are slightly more educated than the average American, but Barna researchers adjusted the representation of college-educated individuals in the weighting scheme accordingly.

The second quantitative online survey was conducted among 508 U.S. Protestant senior pastors from July 25 August 13, 2019. These pastors were recruited from Barna's pastor panel (a database of pastors recruited via probability sampling on annual phone and email surveys) and are representative of U.S. Protestant churches by region, denomination and church size. The margin of error for this sample is +/- 4.2 percent at the 95 percent confidence level.

This study also included ethnographic research and qualitative interviews with 18 individuals who had some kind of experience working with community groups and organizations. These interviews, conducted July–September 2019, used a flexible script to learn how such groups form, how they work and what makes them effective.

Glossary

Gen Z: born between 1999 and 2015
Millennials: born between 1984 and 1998
Gen X: born between 1965 and 1983
Boomers: born between 1946 and 1964
Elders: born between 1945 or earlier

Practicing Christians are self-identified Christians who say their faith is very important in their lives and have attended a worship service within the past month.

GROUP PARTICIPANT DEFINITIONS

- **Community** participants, at some time in their adulthood, have had the following experiences in some kind of group, club or other association:
- Their participation was not required for their education or schooling.
- Their participation was not directly related to their job.
- The group included three or more people.
- The group met three or more times.
- The group provided some external benefit reaching beyond its own participants. Though those benefits might have extended widely, they had to have some local impact, meaning in one's own city or town. Additionally, while a church or Christian community could have benefited, it could not have been the *only* beneficiary of the group's actions.

Barna further defined the spectrum of activity to isolate certain motivations or methods among general participants. These two categories include:

- **Compassionate** participants, who have been involved in at least one group that originated outside of an existing program offered at a church, school, civic or other institution and came together with others to do something they were interested in or passionate about, or in order to change something, help someone or something.
- **Collaborative** participants, who, in addition to being compassionate,

have been involved in at least one group where members shared strong feelings or passions, resources (such as dues, tools or expertise), goals or decision-making abilities. Further, beyond the general prerequisite of having impact in their city or town, respondents had to specifically identify their community as a beneficiary of a group's efforts.

APPENDIX

Acknowledgments

First, Barna Group wishes to thank our partners at Lutheran Hour Ministries, including Ashley Bayless, Jason Broge, Kurt Buchholz, Tony Cook and Don Everts, as well as their team members who participated in pivotal early workshops based on this study's findings. Collaborating on this multi-year project with your ministry has been a joy for our team and a gift to the Church.

We're very grateful for the insights of our expert contributors, both through qualitative study and additional Q&As. Thanks for sharing your thoughts and, more importantly, generously embodying your faith within your spheres of influence. This list includes: Ben Allin, Glenn Barth, Jason Broge, Shawn Duncan, Monica Evans, Ruth Evans, Emily Gibson, Makoto Fujimura, Joy Harty, Lynn Heatley, Scott Kauffman, Gabe Lyons, Kitti Murray, Greg Russinger, Becca Stevens, Stephanie Wieber and Donell Woodson. Lyons also provided helpful input on the scope of the study.

We want to acknowledge some friends of Barna whose books also bear the *Better Together* title and provide tremendous value to the Church: Danielle Strickland, Warren Bird and Jim Tomberlin.

The research team for this project was led by Brooke Hempell and includes Traci Hochmuth, Pam Jacob and Savannah Kimberlin. Kimberlin also provided foundational analysis and data verification for the report. Janet Eason conducted qualitative interviews and ethnographic research. Alyce Youngblood managed the editorial process, and Verónica Thames supported through reporting and interviewing. Doug Brown proofread the manuscript. With creative direction from Joe Jensen, OX Creative designed the cover, and Annette Allen designed interior layout and data visualizations. Brenda Usery managed production. Mallory Holt coordinated as project manager.

Additional thanks for the support of our Barna colleagues: Amy Brands, Daniel Copeland, Aidan Dunn, Aly Hawkins, Kristin Jackson, David Kinnaman, Steve McBeth, Rhesa Storms, Jess Villa and Todd White.

APPENDIX

About the Project Partners

Barna Group is a research firm dedicated to providing actionable insights on faith and culture, with a particular focus on the Christian Church. Since 1984, Barna has conducted more than one million interviews in the course of hundreds of studies, and has become a go-to source for organizations that want to better understand a complex and changing world from a faith perspective. Barna's clients and partners include a broad range of academic institutions, churches, non-profits and businesses, such as Alpha, the Templeton Foundation, Fuller Seminary, the Bill and Melinda Gates Foundation, Maclellan Foundation, DreamWorks Animation, Focus Features, Habitat for Humanity, The Navigators, NBC-Universal, the ONE Campaign, Paramount Pictures, the Salvation Army, Walden Media, Sony and World Vision. The firm's studies are frequently quoted by major media outlets such as *The Economist*, BBC, CNN, *USA Today*, the *Wall Street Journal*, Fox News, *Huffington Post*, *The New York Times* and the *Los Angeles Times*.

Barna.com

Lutheran Hour Ministries is a trusted expert in global media that equips and engages a vibrant volunteer base to passionately proclaim the gospel to more than 100 million people worldwide each week. Through its headquarters in St. Louis, Missouri, and ministry centers on six continents, LHM reaches into more than 50 countries, often bringing Christ to places where no other Christian evangelistic organizations are present.

lhm.org
hopefulneighborhood.org

Go and Tell—But How?

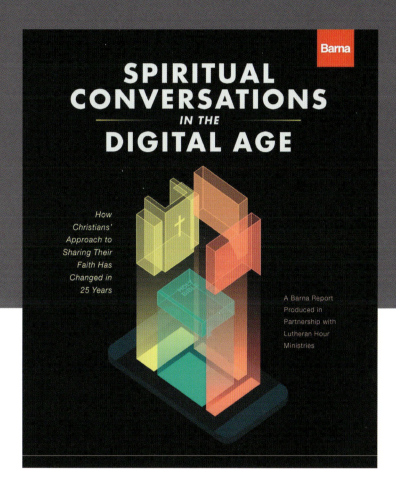

Learn from insights into:

- How priorities and practices have shifted over the past 25 years, including the impact of social media
- Perceptions of faith sharing from both sides of the conversation—the sharer and the hearer
- A data-based profile of eager evangelists
- Generational analysis of today's climate for spiritual conversations

How is our screen-driven society changing the way people talk about their faith? What do people think and feel when they have these conversations? And what can we learn from those Christians who are most active in sharing their faith with others?

This resource helps leaders equip and empower their people with confidence to talk about their faith. Making the connections between everyday, ordinary life experiences and the faith that sustains us brings new inspiration to share the Gospel with others.

Purchase at barna.com/ spiritualconversations

The Rituals and Relationships that Turn a Home into a Sacred Space

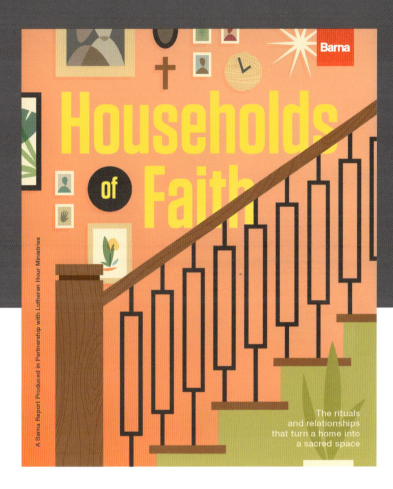

Learn from key findings:

- How peoples' faith heritage is linked to beliefs and rituals in adulthood
- How practicing Christians' core relationships engage them in a thoughtful, transformative faith
- Which practices lead to a spiritually vibrant household with expert insights on how to cultivate faith that lasts

Barna studies have revealed much about the state of religion in the United states and how faith is perceived and discussed in public. But what about how faith is being nurtured in private - with spouses, children, parents, roommates and even frequent visitors who spend time under our roofs?

What does faith look like on a day-to-day basis in practicing Christians' most familiar relationships, personal environments or unobserved hours? With the help of churches, how might that everyday faith become vibrant and enduring?

Purchase at
barna.com/households

☐Barna Access

For you to stay relevant, you have to be informed.

We're excited to announce a new, more affordable way for you to stay current on the best of what Barna is uncovering. It's called Barna Access.

Access is the most innovative way for you to stay informed. It's an exclusive collection of our growing library of research and also includes practical leadership resources.

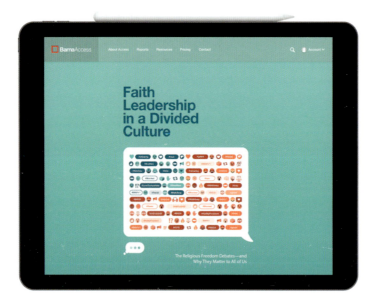

With Access, you'll get:

- All of our best-selling monographs and new reports as they release
- Presentation slide decks that walk through key findings from each report
- Downloadable supporting resources including hundreds of infographics, expert commentaries, video interviews, white papers and articles

Subscribe at access.barna.com